Dancing
THROUGH
DARKNESS

Stories of Healing & Light

KRISTINA COLL
ERMA COOKE
DEBORAH EVANS
TAMARA FAUST
KRIS HANSEN
JULIE POWERS

BALBOA.PRESS
A DIVISION OF HAY HOUSE

Balboa Press books may be ordered through booksellers or by contacting:

Balboa Press
A Division of Hay House
1663 Liberty Drive
Bloomington, IN 47403
www.balboapress.com
844-682-1282

Because of the dynamic nature of the Internet, any web addresses or
links contained in this book may have changed since publication and
may no longer be valid. The views expressed in this work are solely those
of the author and do not necessarily reflect the views of the publisher,
and the publisher hereby disclaims any responsibility for them.

The author of this book does not dispense medical advice or prescribe the use
of any technique as a form of treatment for physical, emotional, or medical
problems without the advice of a physician, either directly or indirectly. The
intent of the author is only to offer information of a general nature to help
you in your quest for emotional and spiritual well-being. In the event you use
any of the information in this book for yourself, which is your constitutional
right, the author and the publisher assume no responsibility for your actions.

Any people depicted in stock imagery provided by Getty Images are
models, and such images are being used for illustrative purposes only.
Certain stock imagery © Getty Images.

This book is a work of non-fiction. Unless otherwise noted, the author
and the publisher make no explicit guarantees as to the accuracy of
the information contained in this book and in some cases, names of
people and places have been altered to protect their privacy.

Print information available on the last page.

ISBN: 979-8-7652-4774-7 (sc)
ISBN: 979-8-7652-4772-3 (hc)
ISBN: 979-8-7652-4773-0 (e)

Library of Congress Control Number: 2023922698

Balboa Press rev. date: 02/20/2024

This book is dedicated to all who are lost in darkness
and are seeking inspiration to dance into the light.

CONTENTS

INTRODUCTION

RESISTANCE & TRUSTING THE UNKNOWN

By Kristina Coll

*O*ur book title is *"Dancing Through Darkness: Stories of Healing & Light."* What is darkness anyway? Is it this black hole we travel through chasing a white rabbit as in "Alice in Wonderland?" We seek the truth of who we are, only to realize that we are ~ who we are: amazing creatures of oneness, stuck in these body suits, trapped by a gravitational pull to earth until the body stops functioning and we take our last breath. Only to awaken and realize that the truth is inside us all along.

The moment I consciously stepped out of darkness was the moment everything became clear. I felt a shift of lightness in my head, a lightness throughout my body that words will never properly express. There was this sense of "settling in" and seeing myself as a golden light in a vast space of nothingness. I was experiencing life from a place entirely different than the one I grew to know and predicted so well; now observing in a way like Neo in *"The Matrix."* No longer was I caught "IN-IT." I was now truly "OF-IT" and watching a beautiful screenplay entirely detached from any form of judgment. I was just purely intrigued with curiosity.

Darkness. The dark? Was I ever afraid of the dark? Nope. Somehow I always knew the darkness was something birthed inside of me. It is intangible. It is not something "out there" or even something done unto me. Darkness is something that I needed to navigate on my own, an inner tapestry woven into this "Human-Suit" and linked with the programming of a computer in my head, the brain. An inner awareness that only I was able to EVER touch, shine a light on, feel in its wholeness and know better than anyone else. *Ahhhhhh*…shining the light in the dark… and I am thinking, "Is there something here?" Yes… Perhaps something we've all heard before and yet didn't always recognize, and so we continued to grasp for understanding.

From birth to age seven, we are our surroundings, our lineage, our past lives, (if you believe there are past lives and/or maybe you've experienced one yourself). DNA is passed from human body to human body; and within this structure, EVERYTHING is stored. From perceptions to disease and anything considered hereditary. During those first years of development, we absorb, observe and *feeeeeel* everything, lacking the understanding of what anything means in our young brains. We store mixed communications that show up in a variety of forms, without the ability to integrate them.

As we grow older, we learn to interpret what particular words mean through the shared language of our society and community. Something as simple as a dictionary defining meaning to words. However, confusion arises when my interpretation of certain communications means one thing based on my personal experiences, and yet the exact same combination of words might mean something entirely different to others based on their experiences. WOW! Now we have a potential mess on our hands, don't we? We may assume that we are aligning with others around us in our understanding of something, when in reality there is misinterpretation and miscommunication stemming from our personal life filters. This is what we call personal perceptions, and it is what creates the breakdowns. The truth underneath, the truth deep within each of us, is an understanding that is entirely NOT the same as anyone else's. Relationships crumble under the weight of the differences, while many bonds can be spared with just a bit more understanding of our differences in life interpretation; with each one of us being open to others' perceptions and becoming more curious in others' experiences. Because of words and feelings being expressed and interpreted entirely differently from one another at early stages of growth in our little minds and bodies, war breaks out inside of us as we battle the understanding within, and thus war can occur outside of us as well. The simplicity of two diverse perspectives can create extreme obstruction to harmony.

It's fascinating to me that even a truly good, pure person can be perceived as a threat when there is a misunderstanding, miscommunication, or lack of shared experience to connect perspectives. Is this the darkness that needs to be explored? Is the darkness the threat? Are we meant to dismantle the entire programming of our youth, our lineages or all of life for that matter, to experience real oneness with everyone around us?

This book is dedicated to all the women who have faced the dark. A true testament to dancing through the darkness and emerging anew. The 'Phoenix Rising from the Ashes' with messages *for* all of us, *from* all of us. Messages of vulnerability, personal truths, experiences, interpretations, and healing. Stories of embracing and embodying the intuitive knowing, and the light, that is within all of us. This book was born in a deep place of darkness and meant to be shared through each author's dance through darkness itself.

How this book began

It was September 2019, and I had traveled to another state to stay with my dear friend and colleague while facilitating some

Spiritual Workshops, and I needed to regroup with myself on a personal transformative experience which I was experiencing. My friend and I participated in a couple of calls we had with the 'Warrior Storytellers' group we had joined a month prior. We had recently joined that group to learn how to write our personal stories and publish a book as a collective sisterhood. We were excited to be part of this life-changing event. This was it! The moment we had been waiting for – a chance to tell our stories of dancing through darkness, transforming and emerging into the light of personal healing and hope for others.

I remember waking up and practicing yoga on the porch that morning; a beautiful, brisk, summer day transitioning into fall weather. I was feeling into the spaciousness of the mountains and the cool breeze. We had another Warrior Storytellers group call scheduled for that day. There we were, hanging out on my friend's terrace, enjoying a cup of coffee, and breathing in the awe-inspiring mountains when I suddenly turned to her and said, "It's a no." She looked at me and instinctively knew exactly what I was talking about, yet proceeded to confirm, "About the book deal?" We had been discussing it a bit and I shared how I simply felt something was *off* about it for me. I caught on early that something was out of alignment with the Warrior Storytellers publisher. I hadn't fully invested yet, and in fact, I had only made my first $250 payment at that point. My investment was minimal, and without hesitation, I canceled myself out of the Warrior Storytellers book deal and chose to fully jump into a book contract with Balboa Press. I had been fence sitting with Balboa for more than a year and this was the push I needed.

After several delays and unkept promises, the book was scheduled to be published in the spring of 2020. There was no reason at that time for the project to dissolve. My friend and another author on that book deal had seen the light and left the project. The publisher "closed the chapter" on the book and claimed Force Majeure for her bankruptcy and she stated in a

Facebook post that her "energy was complete." No funds were returned to the invested authors. The darkness of the experience with this woman blanketed the women's stories meant to bring light to the world.

And then, there it was: a light flickering in the dark. As I was reconnecting with my friend over the phone one day, she shared with me additional details about the obliterated book's backstory, and she shared a little bit about the other four authors' topics. I hadn't yet begun writing my own book; in fact, I wasn't exactly sure what it was going to be about. As my friend was sharing with me, there was a feeling and knowing growing deep down inside of me. This book deal needed to be for *them*. I saw them as women stranded on the side of the road. They each had a story to share of hope and healing, and they also had nowhere to go. They had been fully invested in a dream that had crumbled in front of their eyes, while I had a contract with Balboa Press, hidden to them, but waiting to be revealed. Blood, sweat and tears poured into each of their chapters, and now I could offer an opportunity to merge with them while we all emerged from our ashes to forge our dreams of sharing treasured stories of healing, light and wisdom. This book is for them *and* me. My darkness of resistance had consumed me until I opened this offering to the women who have shared their stories here in this book, and then resistance consumed me once again during the final deadline stretch. What is resistance anyway?

I recently read the book "*The War of Art*," by Steven Pressfield, and *DAMN* was it good! I had never learned about resistance so clearly before this book's outline for recognizing and tearing down barriers. It made so much sense to me, and I saw the resistance in myself. It became even more clear when the women of this book spoke to me as they were experiencing frustration because my resistance manifested itself through not showing up and meeting deadlines for my book submission. I believed I had every legitimate excuse for why it was not complete. I felt that the other authors were being insensitive to my recent move, to living on my own with two small children, to doing my best to thrive when I had desperately found myself simply surviving to get by. I didn't know that resistance works through kids, sickness, death of family members, and unexpected life events popping up out of nowhere. I thought that was simply life happening.

Oh no... no... no.... there it was, resistance showing up in *EVERY* possible way to keep me small, to keep me at amateur status instead of allowing me to become a professional. There I was, poking little fear feathers into the other authors and leaving them to wonder if they would be deserted again. Unknowingly, I was creating doubt in them. Did they think I was the same as the woman from Warrior Storytellers, and perhaps not such a *warrior* at all? Maybe I simply allowed the resistance to invade my head with self judgement because I was NOT showing up and I was not consciously aware yet that I was NOT showing up. This is exactly how "fear" and "doubt" energy can have an adverse effect in our lives and the lives of others with whom we are directly involved. It can butt right up to the others who we are meant to work with. It can create chaos where none was meant to be, and it can prolong the inevitable and maybe even keep us small, insecure.

Once I realized what resistance truly meant and how it shows up for me, I began to integrate the lessons with a pure intention to *be better*, and along the way it can *be messy*. Once I gained awareness that I was playing like an amateur and not a professional, I made the commitment to myself to show up for myself. Right then and there. I truly understand that the more I show up for myself, the more I show up for others along the way. This is what it's like to begin to embody our calling, our passions, our follow-through. With this solid intention and commitment set, trusting the unknown becomes incredibly important as we are guided to places we had never imagined: A secure feeling of knowing that our path is right for us.

Trusting and knowing that we are *ALL* unique with greatness, is a step out of the darkness. Trusting and knowing that everyone has a story, is a step out of darkness. Trusting and knowing that we have the power to heal ourselves, is a step out of darkness. Having pure intentions to do and be better, is a step out of darkness. Placing one's hands over the heart and breathing into this space consciously, intentionally providing love back into self with each breath, is a step out of darkness. Allowing the feelings reaching through the skin of our hands into the depths of our hearts, is a step out of darkness.

Here's to all of you reading these words, all of you who, somewhere along the way, were stranded on the side of the road. When you were - or are - feeling like there is nowhere to go, feeling inadequate, thinking that you are not good enough or not worthy enough and just feeling stuck, now you can read these personal stories of healing and hope. Permit your new faith in your own greatness to keep yourself moving forward through the dark to find the light. YOU are enough. WE are enough. Anything is possible when we believe, trust in the unknown, and face our resistance.

ABOUT THE AUTHOR: KRISTINA COLL

Kristina Coll, 42-year-old mother of two under the age of eight, was born and raised in the Midwest: Iowa, USA. She dove into her personal healing journey and lifelong strengthening inner leadership inner work early in 2012 when a deep sense of "there's more to life than this, and I am done waiting" consumed her. She has experienced many dark nights of the soul. To say there is only one, she'd laugh. She's a fascinating woman whose pure heart, brave soul, gentle spirit, and loyalty to the bigger picture is what keeps her alive. Her greatest lessons being in the areas of 'sustainability' and 'consistency.' She shares a unique perspective on energy, trusting intuition and the unknown, resistance, and its direct connection to relating to others in life. Kristina's thrust in life is 'Believing in Possibilities.' She can be found in a couple of locations as she's dedicated to her transformational intuitive coaching, retreat hosting and breathwork, yoga, meditation, and Reiki facilitation with clients all over the world:

www.heal.me/thelighthouse

www.KristinaColl.com

Youtube Channel: Kristina Coll @kristinacoll7958 'Unfiltered Sensitivity'

Instagram : @iam_kristinacoll

Facebook: https://www.facebook.com/kristinaann.coll/

Facebook: https://www.facebook.com/guidinglightfromwithin/

For virtual yoga, you can find Kristina's classes on the myHealthyYou app under the "Let's Get Movin" section: myhealthyyou.app

ONE

DANCING WITH GRIEF
By Erma Cooke

I was fourteen years, seven months, three weeks and one day old when my life changed forever. It was a beautiful fall day in Georgia. The day began as any other school day in my life. Mom gave us all a good laugh when she swung an outside garbage can at my brother for being a smart aleck when she was "fussing" at him for not taking out the trash. She couldn't yell at him as she could not talk but she got her point across by swinging that garbage can. She waved goodbye until the bus was out of sight on our country dirt road. Just a few minutes later, she would be gone.

I was my mom's "mini-me." As her third daughter, she named me after her, and I was the one who was most like her. She and I had a psychic connection, so no one had to tell me she was gone. I could feel it. When I look back on that day, I realize no one ever did tell me that she was dead. I remember riding home from school that day with my forehead on the cool window and tears rolling down my cheeks knowing in my heart that my mom was dead. I also knew that the responsibility of caring for her was now off my shoulders. I didn't know that grief and over-responsibility would continue to be themes throughout my life.

I was raised in a family where we were taught to *not* show

1

emotions. Anytime I cried, I hid. When I was angry, I stuffed it inside. When I needed to be held, I sought solitude. When I got sad, I reminded myself that she was no longer in pain. I learned, that unless I wanted them to, no one would know what I was feeling. I built up walls to keep everyone out, the tears in, and my deepest, sensitive self, safe. My attitude was "I could take care of others. I could take care of myself. I didn't need anyone's help.

I finished high school and became a Registered Nurse in a newborn nursery. I loved the work, even if it wasn't my first preference. I wanted to be a Pediatric Nurse as I could always connect with kids. After a few years of nursing in a small community hospital, I decided to move to the Regional Hospital and work in the Newborn Intensive Care Unit (NICU).

At the same time, I moved into a live-in, women's drug and alcohol rehabilitation house called Teen Challenge. Teen Challenge is a Christian program for women to come away from the world for a year (three months at our house and then nine months in NY), get sober, create a relationship with God, and then move back into the world.

I had been living at Teen Challenge and working in the NICU for about a year and a half when I started taking care of a baby at work. I'll call him Levi for privacy. Levi was thirteen weeks early and a really sick baby. In his five months in the NICU, he and I developed a special bond. His mom would get aggravated with me when she was trying to get him to open his eyes for her and I could softly whistle across the room and open those eyes would be. His mom and I developed a close relationship as well. Levi finally went home and was doing well, so his mom and I made plans to meet on Monday for lunch and a visit. I had been out of town and came home on Sunday evening. The house was unusually quiet. I was telling the women a funny story about locking my keys in the truck and missing my brother's wedding. They didn't find my story funny, and I thought that was odd. Later that night, the directors of Teen Challenge would tell me that Levi had died early on Saturday morning. I was devastated. All the questions flew through my head like: "What the hell happened?", "How is his mom?", "Where was he when he died?", "Where was she?", and "He was doing so well, how could he be dead?" The next morning I called his mom, and when she found out it was me, she said, "He is dead. It is over. I never want to hear from you again." I was stunned, hurt, and deeply sad. So, true to other deep hurts in my life, I stuffed it behind my emotional walls, didn't process the grief and somehow made myself responsible for her reaction.

Later that week, everyone had gone to church, and I was home alone, praying. Actually, I was yelling at God about the anger I had about Levi dying, about how unfair it was to his mother and to me, and why, just why, did he have to die?! I have a habit of making myself stop and listen after I have been yelling at God. I try to listen to my heart and what it is saying. I heard, "Who are you to say what is and isn't fair? Who are you to live in this house, as an example, asking these women to share their pain with you and you won't share yours with them? If you can't open up with them about this pain, then you need to move on, because you are not the kind of example they need." Ouch! Deep truth! I was asking them to do what I was unwilling to do. As the week continued, they would ask me how I was doing, and I was honest with them about how much it hurt and how sad I was. That Saturday, they went shopping. One of the hardest core women came home with a little grief book called "*I Will Not Leave You Comfortless.*" Immediately, I burst into tears and ran for the kitchen. Those women all came and surrounded me with so much love and concern and held me in ways that I had not been held since my mother died. I understand now, this was the beginning of my healing journey in life.

These are two of the examples of ways I have danced with grief in my life. A few years ago, I was introduced to Laura Jack, a Compassion Coach with a vision to create an Army of

Compassion in this world. Not knowing why, I decided to take her Compassion Code Academy coaching class. In this four-month, on-line class, I learned how much a lifetime of healing can change a person, and so much more. I learned the following definition of grief used by the Grief Recovery Institute: "Grief is the conflicting feelings caused by the end of, or change in, a familiar pattern of behavior." What I fully understood upon hearing this definition was that I had danced with grief so many times in my life, in ways which I didn't identify as grief.

In January of 1994, I found myself back at the community hospital where I had started my nursing career. I was starting my Neonatal Nurse Practitioner (NNP) career as the first Nurse Practitioner hired by the hospital outside of Nurse Midwives. I knew transitioning into a different position as a provider and not a nurse was going to be difficult, especially as the only NNP. After I completed my job description, the Chief of Pediatrics asked me to rewrite the physician orders to comply with newer order sets I had encountered in NNP school. My deadline for creating this order set and having it on the books was the end of February. The next week the Director of Nursing came to my office and instructed me to rewrite all the policies to match the order sets. We had an in-depth conversation about the role of an NNP versus the role of a Nurse Manager and Assistant Nurse Manager. I felt in my new role I had to set some boundaries. When the Joint Commission survey was moved to the first week of April, those boundaries went out the window. I, along with several members of the staff, cleaned, created, wrote and requested all the equipment we needed to pass the Joint Commission survey. We passed the Joint Commission Survey with flying colors. At the end of the week, the CEO of the hospital gave kudos to the Head Nurse for being the only place in the hospital that didn't have any findings. I was angry and frustrated, so I quietly walked out of the meeting, took my pager to the nursery and told the staff to put up a note that I was not taking any calls until Tuesday after I completed my NNP Board exams.

A group of us traveled to Atlanta to take different certification exams. I knew as I walked out of the exam that I did not pass it. I also knew that in not passing it, in the state of Georgia, I could no longer work as an NNP. In June, my thoughts were confirmed as I did not pass my Certification Exam. I went to the Director of Nursing and shared the news. She immediately demoted me to staff nurse on night shift. I went home that day disappointed that she did not make me an Assistant Nurse Manager so I could continue to work on the programs I had started as an NNP. When I went to see a friend/mentor of mine, he asked me if I had failed the test on purpose as the work situation up to that point had been horrible. Looking back, though I denied it at the time, the answer was *yes*. I was so angry, disappointed, and frustrated by being made the "responsible one" and not being given credit for my accomplishments that I set myself up to fail as a way to blame others and get out of a depressing situation.

There was deep grief around this move, as I was leaving my dreams for my future work as an NNP in a small community hospital. I was leaving a group of friends that I was beginning to let inside my walls. I was leaving a community where I was being seen as a leader not only in neonatal care but in the community at large. As was my pattern, I pushed all the grief behind the walls and moved on to my next adventure as an NNP in a large city hospital in Colorado where they didn't require the same certification. (Without the pressure, I was actually able to pass the certification test before I made the move, so I was prepared for any future adventure.)

After a few months in Colorado, I had a crisis of faith. One day I found out that a friend had lied to me about something that was really important to both of us. To this day, I don't remember what she lied about. The lie was the catalyst for my next "come to Jesus" conversation with God. I was angry with her for lying to me, and I was angry with myself for trusting her and being hurt by her. I let her inside my walls, and she hurt me. True to my nature, that night I was yelling at God about it. I was hurt, and I was taking it out on my relationship with God. Also true to my nature, when I finished yelling and being angry, I waited. What I heard was...

God: "You are one to be hurt by people lying to you. You lie every day of your life!"
Me - clueless: "Um, excuse me. What do I lie about every day?"
God: "Your sexuality."
Me – cringing: "I didn't think I could be gay and a Christian."
God: "Who told you that?"

I have to say I stopped listening at that point. If God was challenging me to be the person He made me to be, then how did that reconcile with years of church teachings that "If you are gay, you are in sin and need to repent from your sins." I just couldn't wrap my head around it, and I couldn't continue living the way I was living either. I walked away from the job, the friends, and the church. I took a job half a country away where no one knew me, and I could work on what it meant to live out my life as a gay woman. How did that fit into what I had learned at the church? If what the church had taught me about homosexuality was wrong, then what about all the other beliefs I had? The ones about being called to my profession, about being a facilitator of healing, about dreaming dreams for the world and about Jesus and the church. Just exactly what did all those teachings mean and what was left? What would the church people I had worked with side-by-side do and say when I came out and broke my silence? I fully came out in 1998, and I found out the answer to my question from people I loved dearly, worked alongside doing the "work of God," and had been friends with for years. I lost a big part of my extended family during those years. However, I had a group of friends who stood by me, and some of them came out as well. Others in the group held space for us to process, talk and work through what it meant to be gay in the Deep South, and in churches that didn't accept being gay. Two of us were on the leadership team for a weekend retreat which met yearly at Saint Simons Island, Georgia, with a group called Faith at Work. We helped run that retreat for years, and the last few years I was honored to be the Chairperson for the retreat. It was one of the few places where I was safe to dive in to learn about myself and God in different ways. Today I sit on the Board of Directors of Lumunos (formally known as Faith at Work) as a way to give back to a community that gave so much to me, as I was learning to grow and live outside those walls of protection and learning what was my responsibility.

As I moved around the country trying to find a safe place to land, I got into a long-distance relationship with the woman who would become my first partner. We talked on the phone for hours, visited when we could work it into our schedules and finally decided to move in together. She had a seventeen-year-old son with whom I was developing a growing relationship due to working together to find our home in Maryland. His mom was not a part of these times, and when we found a place to live, we let her know. She was blessed that I was creating a bond of love with her son as we developed our relationship.

As my partner and her son were driving across the country in a refurbished 1967 Barracuda, they were in an automobile accident. I got "the" call after coming off a night shift. My partner was standing on the side of the road telling me that her son wasn't moving, and they were breathing for him. My heart broke. When I arrived at the Shock Trauma Unit, the nurse asked me how I was related, and I couldn't think of an answer. I finally told her, "His mom and I are partners and there is a letter in his chart that gives me permission to know all about his care and what is going on with him." She filled me in, and the news was as horrific as I thought it was going to be. He had a closed-head injury, ruptured diaphragm, bruised lungs, and his heart was pumping at 15%. His outcome didn't look good. Here I was, alone in his room, trying to digest the information that this young man who I was learning to love, may not make it. When his mom arrived later that night, I met her in the hallway, and she asked how he was. All I could do was say, "This is not good. He is in really bad shape." As she leaned into my hug, she wept. Our friends, who had picked her up and brought her to Salt Lake City, were all in shock. There were so many moments of gut-wrenching shock, grief and sadness in the days that followed. By day six, we knew he had a severed spinal cord and would never wake up. His only sign of life was an occasional sighing breath. We were keeping his friends in our community up to date on his condition when we received a letter from his friends. They wrote us and asked us not to make him a "vegetable in a nursing home." Shortly after we received this letter, all the family was gathered and was asked to take him off life support, and to donate his organs and tissues. We agreed and took him off life support a few days later.

Those days in the hospital were unimaginable! For me, I just kept stuffing the feelings and emotions behind my wall and remained the "responsible one." Grief was once again knocking on the door to my heart. I then reached out to someone I thought could support me in this time, but that person was not able. This just buried the grief deeper inside the walls.

Shortly after my stepson's death, my work life was at its lowest point. I had trauma from seeing my stepson in that hospital bed that bled over into my work. One night I was talking to a mother who was being asked to take her daughter off life support. In her angst, she told me that no parent ever had to make that decision. I sat with her and shared our story. The next morning, my boss got upset with me for talking to her. I immediately put in my ninety-day notice and decided this "NNP stuff" just wasn't for me. I was smart enough to figure out a different life path and would do so.

A month or so later, I walked into the NICU and went to a

little three-pound guy's bed. As I lifted the cover so I could see him, he looked up at me with big chocolate eyes, and I felt deep in my being "And you think you can leave us?" My soul's resounding response was "NO!" I knew from that point on, I would always be an NNP at heart. I moved on to find a nursery where I could use my gifts for teaching, mentoring, and communicating.

After settling into our new home and jobs, we decided to take a vacation just for us. The first day we were there, I was anxious and out of sorts. It bothered my partner and when she questioned me, I told her that I didn't know what wasn't right, but something was really wrong in my world. I just couldn't figure out what. We were just settling in that night when one of my dearest friends called me to tell me her son had been shot and killed in a gun accident. As I was weeping while talking with her on the phone, my partner got up and packed our belongings, loaded our truck, and checked us out of the hotel. I asked her what she was doing, and she said, "You are going to be with your friend. I am going to take you there. She needs you." I didn't want to go, as this was a family who was having difficulty with me being gay. I told her we could just go up for the funeral on Thursday. She wouldn't take my "no" for an answer.

I did a lot of "taking care" with my friends that week. I also had two very healing conversations. The first was about how life puts everything else into perspective, and the second was about how important it was for me to be there for them during this time. I told my friend I was there because my partner made me come. After we finished talking, she went in and thanked my partner for bringing me to them. Those conversation were the beginning of healing in our relationship.

A few years ago, my friend and I talked on the phone for the better part of an afternoon about our stories of how we were alone when we heard the news of our boys and traveled halfway across the country to get to our families. Another step in healing for our hearts and our relationship. Today as I write this with tears flowing down my cheeks, I realize I did what I was really good at when my young friend died. I stuffed my feelings, took care of everyone else, and did not do my own grieving. I now know the tears I stuffed back are toxic to my body, so I choose to let them flow freely.

What I didn't realize at the time was this death had triggered my partner, and she was spiraling into a deep depression and anger over her own loss. Over the next few years, problems I was having at work, her son's death and problems in our relationship caused me to end the relationship. At some point near the end, my therapist had us both in a session, and my partner exploded on me. I shrank into the chair I was sitting in, froze and threw up all the walls I had learned to take down. My trust was broken, and I realized I could not live in the same house with someone who broke my trust. At the same time, the problems at work came to a head, and I resigned my job and moved to another city where I didn't know anyone so that I could try to heal from my brokenness. However, this time I was in isolation and relying on myself, and not the network of people who I had learned to let in. What I have learned is that when I isolate and tell myself that "I can take care of it all myself" or "I don't need anyone else," those statements are my trauma responses. We all need people in our lives to help us through the rough spots, to talk to, and to hold safe space for us to explore who we are now and how to heal broken places in our hearts.

Less than a year later, when my dad had a severe transient ischemia attack (TIA) (like a stroke but without long term repercussions), I realized that he was getting older, and I wanted to live near the family so that I could visit him occasionally, and to be available if he were to get sick again. Over the years, Dad and I had come to a place in our relationship where we could spend time together and enjoy one another's company. We had running jokes no one understood, and my siblings couldn't quite figure out our relationship. I found a job closer to home, in North Carolina, and one of my brothers came to Texas to help me move.

During that time, I started dating the woman who would become my second partner and then legally my wife. My dad was determined to be at our wedding even though his health was failing. He cried when he sat beside the memorial I made for my mom, and he wouldn't let us take a picture with him sitting in his wheelchair. He wanted me to remember him as a strong man. I realized that day where I got some of my strength and determination – from my dad.

In December 2009, I got a call from my brother telling me dad had passed away that morning. I will never forget it because I wasn't expecting it, and it struck me deeply. The tears flowed. My brother was calling from the funeral home because in Georgia all family members have to say it is okay for the person to be cremated. He then asked what kind of urn I would like for him. I replied, "I don't care." He asked me again emphasizing "What do YOU want?" I had a good belly laugh as dad had changed his will to leave his ashes to me. He did that because one day I was giving him grief about not telling us what to do with them. I told him that as his youngest daughter, I had made an executive decision that when he died, I was going to find the biggest bottle of Hennessy Cognac I could find, we would drink it in his honor and then I was going to pour his ashes in it and throw it on the shelf so he could be with us always. After I hung up, I looked up and told him that he certainly got the last laugh, and I promised him that I would not leave his ashes on the shelf. My sadness at his passing would wash over me in waves in the coming months. About six months later, I created a ceremony for my siblings, my extended family, and for me to say goodbye to him. The ritual of ceremony honored who he was, his favorite things, and our relationship with him. It provided me another space to safely move through my grief over his death.

Shortly after his death and while continuing to grieve, I

was offered an opportunity to move to Germany and work at the American Military Hospital. I had lived in Germany for a year in high school, and my wife had lived there for several years. We decided to take the job and explore Europe in ways we had never dreamed. We packed our bags, said goodbye to dear friends and family, and headed to Germany. Although this was an exciting move, there was still sadness and grief at leaving friends who had a special place in our hearts. Those three years in Germany were filled with many fun times, challenging times, and grand adventures. In the end, we were ready to come back home.

In 2014, we moved from Germany, where I worked as Medical Director of Newborn Nursery and as a NNP in the ten bed NICU to Asheville, NC where I would be an NNP in a fifty-three bed Neonatal Intensive Care Nursery (NICU). Working in a NICU that size is daunting at best for an empath. I knew I would need to find ways to set boundaries with families, staff, and, not surprisingly, my personal life. The first project I was asked to be part of was the Neonatal Abstinence Committee. This was a multidisciplinary group deciding how to provide the best care for our neonates whose mothers were either addicted to opiates or who were on maintenance opiates to help their addiction problems. I served on that committee for four years and learned a lot about addiction, neonatal withdrawal and what everyone, (staff included), goes through when the baby is born. I learned that if I could deeply center and calm myself, I could help the babies calm themselves. If I wasn't centered and calm, I wasn't very helpful to those babies. I learned to calm myself with breathing exercises, silence, and imagining myself deeply rooted in the earth along with other techniques.

There is so much grief in the NICU, and the staff taking care of these babies are daily putting their own grief aside to hold space for the patients' families. The walls I was learning to take down were very useful in the times when a baby died, an emergency surgery had to be done on a favorite patient, an outcome was not what we expected, and all the other peaks and valleys of being in a NICU. The dance was to change those walls into containers that could hold grief, allow the grief to be poured out when appropriate and create safety for everyone.

Later, I was asked if I would go to one of the outlying hospitals and help with Newborn Nursery coverage. I was the only NNP in the system who had extensive Newborn Nursery experience and was known, by that time, to be a good teacher. My charge was to "cover the newborn service, teach the nurses how to care for a sick baby and participate on all the Newborn Policy and Procedure Committees between the community hospitals and the regional center." After six months of part-time work, I was asked to go to that community hospital full time. The timing was perfect as my marriage was falling apart and I thought the space might help us work on our problems. What I didn't know was that I would be working twenty-six days out of the month. I was promised that help would be coming, and when we hired and trained the new staff, I could come back to the regional hospital and work in the newborn nursery with the Neonatal Abstinence babies.

I spent eighteen months working this schedule without any help in sight. Each time we had a plan, it fell through. I taught the nurses several classes relating to caring for newborns in a community hospital. I developed a newborn telemedicine program so the nurses and providers in the community hospital could talk to the NICU, and the NICU providers could see the babies and direct the patients' care. I sat on every committee. My marriage continued to fall to pieces. Early one morning, I got a phone call from the nurses: "We need you now! We have 29-week twins who are going to deliver!" I threw on my scrubs and got to the hospital in record time. On the way, I called the NICU to see who would be on the telemedicine call and see how quickly we could get a NICU team. The provider sent the NICU team via helicopter, and the second team via ambulance. When I got to the hospital, I was thankful for all the work I had done, as my nurses had everything set up and ready to go. The NICU team got there just as the first baby was being born. We stabilized baby "A," and the second team got there just after baby "B" was born. The provider was on telemedicine for delivery and stabilization. I was OVERJOYED. The nurses were amazing. The system we put in place worked better than I could have dreamed. I spent the next week bragging to everyone in administration about how the nurses functioned, how the telemedicine worked, and how helpful it was to have the NICU team there from the beginning. I was elated to go on an extended, much needed vacation knowing the staff had everything under control.

The second week into my vacation, I got a text from the obstetrics manager "Call me ASAP!" My heart sank, as I knew something serious had happened. Later that morning, I called her and learned that the Regional Hospital that owned our community hospital had just announced to the staff that the Obstetrics Unit would be permanently closing and the nurses who could not find jobs within the hospital would be laid off. I was in shock, heartbroken, and angry. Why had I done all that work for the better part of three years for them to just shut it all down?!? I didn't hear the news from my boss until Thursday afternoon. When I asked if I would be allowed to come back to the Regional Hospital for the promised job, her answer was "There is no job for you here." In my thirty plus years of nursing, I had never imagined that I would be laid off. There I was with three months to find a job, move, and settle into a new community. It was a daunting process since I knew as an NNP it would take at least two to four months for me to find a job and get credentialed. I knew I had at least four to six months of unemployment ahead of me.

The anger and grief I felt about investing so much of my time, energy and knowledge to this unit was alternating between overwhelming and mind numbing. I worked hard, as did every nurse, tech, obstetrician, and pediatrician, to make this small community hospital "the" place in our area to delivery your baby. We had done it. Our service was growing, and we had the reputation we wanted. In one sweep of the administrative hand, it was all gone, without an honest answer about why. Everyone's life was changed. Some nurses left obstetrics, some travelled to continue the careers they loved, and some stepped out of nursing all together. One thing we were all sure about was that we were not participating in a "party" the system wanted to give us. We were all just too angry.

Having danced with grief so much in my life, I knew that having some ceremony of closure would be vital for all of us to move on from this loss. I knew we needed to celebrate all that we had accomplished in that community. I created a "Celebrating our Successes" party. We invited the community, the staff, the administration from the hospital, and the providers. We gathered. We handed out funny, serious, amazing awards to each of the providers, nurses, and support staff. At some point during the party, one of the nurses walked up to me and said, "Erma, this is not a failure on your part. Remember, just because we won't be working together doesn't mean we will forget all you taught us. We will carry all that knowledge into the community hospitals where we go, and we will teach others." She gave me a big hug as tears streamed down both of our cheeks. Her words gave me a personal moment of peace in this deeply felt loss.

In addition to losing my job, I finalized my divorce agreement. I felt like my whole world had imploded around me, and I was just barely able to stay afloat. I was moving again for the third time in four years. I was giving up the two schnauzers we had for ten years. I let my ex have most of our joint possessions and spent many days dealing with our problems. Life was sad, hard, and felt very harsh at that moment. I found I had resources to help me through. I had friends whom I called A LOT. I had an amazing therapist. I was in a group of women with a coach who was teaching us all kinds of ways to help us deal with stress, overwhelm and burnout in our lives. I was starting a new job where I was going to be using the technology I had helped set up at my old job. I was moving to live near one of my lifelong friends. We had never lived close to each other, and I was thrilled to be in the same town. I had a few months off to travel, refill and refuel before I started my next job as the first NNP in a larger community hospital.

I started my job in the fall on the tail of two Category 5 hurricanes. I joked with the CEO about the odds of having two hurricanes named a variant of my name. Hurricane Irma roared through Georgia followed closely by Hurricane Maria. He laughed until he realized I was serious, and then he was suspiciously quiet. I loved the doctors and other NNPs at the hospital but was not happy with how the Newborn Service was running, and the initial response from a few of the nursing staff. I would learn over time those same few nurses were always at the center of any controversy in or about the new program we were trying to set up. I realize now they were grieving their own loss of how things had been done in their NICU and Nursery and how their jobs were shifting. We all respond to grief and change differently; some of us acknowledge it and others fight it with all they have in hopes that things will go back to "normal." After four months of having one NNP after another refuse to work with this group, I threw in the towel myself and started looking for a job.

Though work life was tough, home life was peaceful. It was a healing environment, and for the first time in a long time, I was happy with my personal life. It was so much fun to have friends nearby, people to hang out with in the evenings, random phone calls for a quick lunch, and food brought to me when I was sick. I thrived in the quiet nights putting together puzzles, writing during the days, and having deep conversations. I was enjoying the closing months of a nine-month coaching class and using the things I learned to shift and heal so many areas in my life.

With home life being so peaceful, I was angry when I realized I didn't want to uproot myself one more time. I also realized it was a choice I was making – to not allow myself to become burnt out at work and shift to a healthier work environment. I would miss being so close to my friends, but knew I had such a healing time while I was there. My friend would later tell me I had changed the negative energy in the house where she grew up into positive energy, and she loved it.

I went back to a small community hospital that needed pediatric coverage. I wouldn't be the only NNP there, as they had already hired one. He and I are a good working pair, as I like administrative processes and he likes problem solving and policy writing. I work less than I ever have and enjoy the staff and the work. I don't take care of sick babies much these days, but when I do, I make sure to talk to the moms about what it's like to have a baby in the NICU and options for handling grief and self-care. Those are important discussions.

This work schedule allowed me to move my beloved, feisty, ninety-year-old aunt to North Carolina from New Jersey to live near me. When she fell and broke her hip, she told the orthopedic surgeon he was going to fix it, as she wasn't spending the rest of her life in bed. We moved her to an apartment which was set up for elderly people. It was a safe place for her to land now that she wasn't fully able to take care of herself, and it was great for me as it was just down the hill from the hospital. I checked on her often, took her out for meals and appointments, and managed her accounts so she wouldn't forget to pay the important bills. For the first time in my life, I was able to just drop in and see her instead of having to make a journey.

When Covid 19 hit, we threw her birthday parties via Zoom, but there were no more spontaneous lunches or outings. We talked on the phone often. As her dementia worsened, I had to be vigilant about answering my phone or she would think something bad had happened to me. I think the combination of worsening dementia and the isolation of Covid 19 created more anxiety for both of us.

As the country started opening more, and we could visit more in person, I was more aware of the dementia. I quit my second job to be at home and be more attentive. I consulted her physician and had her final wishes put on an outpatient "Do Not Resuscitate" order. I was so thankful we had those hard discussions before I was concerned about her dementia. She had never been married, and as I continued to help her adjust to a life where she had to depend on someone else, I learned where I got more of my stubborn independence from. I consulted Palliative Care and was so thankful for their help and input. I was losing my favorite aunt a little more each day, and I was out of my element. I was grieving while trying not to be overly responsible.

One afternoon when she was having a cogent moment, she, my brother, and I talked about her dying. She told us she was ready to go, and she had no regrets. We told her when she was ready, to please go. I reassured her that I would bury her in New Jersey. It was really important for us to have that conversation. We had no doubt she was ready, and she had no doubt that we were okay with her dying. Within three weeks of that conversation, she passed away peacefully in the Hospice House under the skillful care of the Hospice Nurses, with her favorite rosary in her hand. Her passing was one of those times in life where I clearly saw the "both/and" of life. I was happy that she was no longer suffering from dementia and not herself, and I was sad that she was gone. I missed her every day. I found myself waiting for the phone to ring around six o'clock every evening. I asked myself if I needed to stop and check on her only to remember she wasn't there. I danced with my grief very differently than I had at any other time in my life. I allowed my brother to take care of me. I asked my friends to come up for the service. I asked one of my friends to come to New Jersey for her funeral. I leaned into my support and not away from it. The tears flowed when I was with people and when I was alone. I realized that I had learned to look at, and feel, grief differently.

Over the next several months I was challenged by my new way of grieving as my best friends lost their grandson in a motorcycle accident, and as I assisted my nieces and nephew in the final care of my oldest sister as she was in the ICU dying of Covid 19 complications. I found I had the support I needed, the resources I needed, and the inner strength to feel the grief and not push it all inside. I found those walls I had built still had some remnants. I think they always will. I have learned skills to prevent those remnants from allowing me to express who I am and help me to hold space for other people to express who they are. In dancing with my grief, I have found ways to be responsible for my emotions, not be overly responsible in caring for everyone at the detriment of myself, and how to be gentle with myself when the waves of grief wash over me.

What does the next chapter hold? Who knows? However, I do know that the Covid 19 pandemic brought so much grief into my world and the world at large. I see that I went into survival mode during the pandemic. The definition of grief from the Grief Recovery Institute is "the conflicting feelings caused by the end of or change in a familiar pattern of behavior." I know the world went into the same survival mode. We lost so much to this horrible disease and were not able to process those losses in healthy ways. I was finding friends in a new community, and we could no longer meet. I traveled a lot before the pandemic, but not anymore. My work didn't change, but the way I did my work changed dramatically. I keep hearing people say, "I can't wait to get back to normal." There is no going back from this, only forward. My deepest desire is to move forward into a more compassionate life. My prayer for myself and for the world is for us to find a way to dance with the grief in our daily lives, to find grief not as a feared or avoided topic, but as a natural part of our world. I see a world where we create spaces where grief can be acknowledged with love and compassion, and where tears are as natural as laughter. A space where there is no place for the walls, allowing people to be gentle with one another. A space that allows all the toxic tears we have held in for so long to flow freely.

This chapter is dedicated to my mentor, friend and adopted big sister, Kay Campbell. Shortly after Kay completed editing this chapter, she was diagnosed with a fast-growing brain cancer. I am so thankful to have had her in my life and a big part of this project.

ABOUT THE AUTHOR: ERMA COOKE

Erma Cooke is a Neonatal Nurse Practitioner who has a passion for growing, learning, and teaching. She worked as a Registered Nurse from 1984 to 1994 and Neonatal Nurse Practitioner from 1994 to present. She enjoys traveling and lived in Germany for three years taking care of babies of military service members. Her ability to sit with her own grief has made her a remarkable companion for people as they work with the grief in their lives.

TWO

DANCING THROUGH BROKENNESS
By Deborah Evans

"And in the valley beneath the mountains of my youth, lies the river of my tears. As it wends its way to the ocean of my dreams so long ago, they have gone… Then I must not supply this endless fountain that creates the river of my tears but look beyond those mountains where the **bluebird of happiness** flies." George J. Carroll, *A Journey from Pain to Peace*

*T*oday one in three women is affected by sexual trauma in her lifetime. That is one-third of us at least. Once in our family trees, sexual wounding somehow keeps getting passed down from one generation to the next, just like the "secret family recipe" does. Sexual trauma is a recipe for disaster – a generational legacy of close encounters of the worst kind. After more than five long decades of sexual injuries, I found myself still living in Victimhood, on Suffering Street, in a house of brokenness painted in shame. I felt inadequate, damaged, defective, unlovable, untouchable.

Despite all my efforts to keep my daughter safe, she's been drastically affected and imprinted now too. Left unhealed, there's self-abandonment, self-punishments, isolating, panic attacks, illnesses, suicide attempts and the everyday struggles to function. Plus, more, including finding abusive relationships and romantic partners and missing out on healthy, loving relationships. I love my daughter and I don't want this for her life! I want her to live her life fully! Starting now. Not in her fifties! How do we stop this? How do we heal ourselves beyond it?

Many moons ago, I began wondering, "What about me is attracting all that?" When I checked in with myself, I exuded the energy of "prey." Written all over me were "weak and worthless." I had attracted these incidents like a lamb attracts the hungry wolf.

In my house in the late 1970s there seemed to be a "Don't Ask, Don't Tell" policy. My mother didn't ask, and I didn't tell. By my fourteenth year, and a move from the poor indentured-servant, immigrant part of town to cookie-cutter house suburbia, silence was the golden rule in my family. My life seemed to fare much better when I just kept my thoughts and feelings to myself. Many times, I accepted my "inadequacy and idiocy" as the problem, so any issue would just boil over and be done. Anything for peace. "Yes, I did it," I always agreed even if I hadn't. I knew right away that "it" was all my fault. Everything about last night would be attributed to my doings, my conjuring, my deserved sufferings. I knew it would need to be shoved under that proverbial rug, hidden from all forever, never to be spoken of again. Was there enough shag carpet to cover my shame? I felt that no justice was going to be had for me. No one was going to stand up for me. Who did I think I was anyway? I was born to teenage parents in the 1960s who dropped out of ninth grade just to bring me into the world. My existence already didn't exude bluebird happiness and melodies of birdsong joy to them. Times were tough. I love you, I'm proud of you, and hugs were scarce.

The question was, "Well, what did *you* do?" That familiar question insinuating that whatever happened was, indeed, always my fault. That was the given in the equation of what my ensuing punishment would be of switches, bullwhips, and belt buckles. I was scared out of my schoolgirl wits. I knew the whole world would have to change if I told and I was terrified of that. And I felt disgusting. I was a whirlwind of uncertainty, a little girl lost. I wished I were dead.

One day right before my first day of tenth grade, I sauntered down the road in the blue-gold dusk of autumn in my new waitress uniform of a red t-shirt and a red baseball hat which became the worst night of my life. It was the first time I saw red. The first time I hated red. That Friday night was four months after my Daddy left home with his young mistress, so I immediately started working for survival, dance training, and college later. With a future of regular paychecks in my back pocket, I literally started skipping like a little girl down the sidewalk to my first work party truly believing everything's going to be okay. Instead, I got my virgin, waiting-till-marriage, Christian-self, drugged and sexually assaulted.

This movie night at the work party, I was given a sweet, liquid, peppermint ambrosia in a large, vintage coke glass with no idea that it was alcohol. After the movie, I stood up to go to the restroom with a swimmingly slow motion, grasping air for support. I collapsed, smashing my head on the oak coffee table. My ignorance and naiveté did not serve me well on that night. I crumpled like a wingless bird that has fallen from the sky. No control. No strength. Dead weight. Not aware. Not consenting either. Pushed out of the nest of privacy and personal boundaries. Caught in the snare of the hungry wolf in sheep's clothing. I go black. My innocence and trust just gone as fast as the whirlwind blows. At some point I must've been taken outside, tossed, turned, and rolled around on the wet ground and then brought back inside. I was broken and violated in the darkness of that night. I went home muddy, grass in my hair, scratched and bruised, disheveled, and late to work. Work called my home and then mother called that house. The ringing of that phone struck like a chord played by the devil himself to awaken me to my reality.

I was half-naked, lying on the shag carpet of that floor feeling shame. I didn't remember much yet.

On that day in the sweltering heat of August 1979 in a suburb of Houston, Texas, I mentally split in two. I became two girls. The defective and disgusting girl was to carry it all in her blood-red purse of spilled perfume who's keeping a web of tangled shame hidden deep within her purse pockets. It would be the first day I couldn't bear myself, that ugliness that even a scalding shower couldn't erase. I worked all day with him, the older boy that violated me. I vomited six times. My blood was boiling with fever, my body burning with disgust that was left on me and in me. I was stained as red as my work clothes, but I smiled and acted as if it were fine. Knowing I am on my own totally and I'm the only one I can count on, I engulf myself in school, making good grades for college scholarships. I danced my tail feathers off, leaving a trail of secrets and tears behind on the darkened cold floor of my lonely, blank stage.

A clean slate and a white satin prom gown with the love of my young life, a handsome football player with the sun shining right through him and his thick hair. He is golden. We climbed a mountain together, touching the blue sky at the top of the world, dreaming of our future beyond the vast horizon. Suddenly, my "golden-hair" boyfriend and I broke up. I was devastated. I wasn't used to being so close to someone. I couldn't tell him what happened to me. I was triggered and scared, and he had been my ride home from work. As I was walking home a customer drove up alongside and gave me a ride. He told me he secretly watched me competitively swim for years. I saw red again. I realized he wasn't leaving me alive when his sweaty hands squeezed around my neck. I prayed and forced myself to stop breathing, to stop fighting under the crushing weight of him. I blacked out. He literally pushed me out of his truck and left me for dead, skinning me up on the cement sidewalk. Playing dead saved my life.

This time I put my big girl panties on and called for help. I called the police even though I was not used to asking for help. In my family, you don't ask for help. The policeman who came wasn't much older than I was. He said, "You're too pretty," looking me up and down, "Yeah, you're too pretty and why would you be out here at 11:00 P. M. all alone? Where are your parents?" I was flabbergasted. What does "too pretty" mean? I'm in greasy jeans, red t-shirt, and baseball hat, smelling like a French fry. I'm still at the same restaurant for seven years now. Also, I'm a maid and a radiology receptionist at the hospital working my way through college and helping my paralyzed Grandma on Sunday mornings. For free I sing to the deaf in sign language. The young policeman talked to me firmly, "Young lady, let's not catch you out here alone late at night again. Find a ride." After telling the police about the perpetrator's red truck and his name nothing ever came of it. Later, I realized that I wasn't even worth a police report. I didn't warrant a doctor examination or evidence collection either. No investigation. So much for getting up the courage to call for help; I can't even get it from a policeman. I was nothing. I believed I was worth less than the trash on a cement sidewalk. I was loathing my body, hating myself. I was questioning God. A decade later I saw that the policeman posted sexually explicit material on the internet and was no longer on patrol.

I dropped my college summer classes and hid away at my boss's house while my injuries healed. I became afraid I'd be blamed somehow. So, I steamed up the hot water, scalded myself clean for many months and buried this shame in that bloody red purse. Not mine, of course - I'm mastering blocking out that which I can't handle. Besides, I have had too much to do to simply survive. I was also bitten by a blood-sucking tick at eighteen during the mountain adventure of my lifetime and was having seizures. I lost thirty pounds in one month and was down to 88 pounds. The college "quack shack" considered that I had ringworm, and I was misdiagnosed. I was so sick, and my new task was just to live. Then when I went back to college, I became reckless and started running at a track at 11:00 P.M. at night alone.

I kept daring God to take me. Maybe I was trying to escape from reality? Maybe I was trying to prove it wasn't going to affect me or destroy me? Maybe I wanted to prove I was in charge, that I still was in control? It was really bothering me. This secret. Again. I was loathing my body, hating myself for all these happenings. I was beginning to believe it really was my fault. I was stressed and overthinking for years. These hauntings, questioning God too and why the hell did He leave when my daddy left?

My "golden-hair" boyfriend and I reunited. We were twenty-one, our future looked bright, and college graduation was near. The best day of my life would be on a lake in a canoe when, with the golden sun warm on our backs, he listened to my dreams, and I listened to his. The leaves in the wind were blowing peace all around us. Only we existed. Soon one forsaken night, a trusted friend of my "golden-hair" boyfriend gave me a ride, and then sexually assaulted me. He pushed me out of his moving car, skinning me up on the gravel parking lot. So, this frazzled "little girl" freaked out. I felt that I just didn't matter. I shouldn't be taking up air that someone else would breathe better. That I was disgusting, and gross, would echo in my head for decades until life shook me to my core.

Then after five years of silently fighting in HPV16/18 cervical cancer shame, with fourteen surgeries and treatments, I beat the cancer at age twenty-six. Another man proposed and offered me a diamond ring. This sparkly carat of love had a hidden price. I lived in terror that at any moment he would force himself on me. He won't take "no" for an answer. I learned to just lay there and get the sex act over with. He didn't even care that I was stiff as a dead doll. I felt a dangerous red overcome me. That became my worth as a woman, as a human. I felt powerless, helpless, and hopeless. Abused and codependent were now labels on my coat of many colors. Trauma bonded, I left him two weeks before the wedding when he broke into my apartment and threatened to shoot me, drunkenly pointing a rifle at me. The outcome of his final wrath would be property damage - holes in the walls, a broken chair, a cracked bar, a broken coffee table. All because I asked him to make his own sandwich after I worked all night. Goodbye, my fiancée, my violator of choice.

Next, on my way to dance to "True Blue" by Madonna and a few other songs at a Fashion and Bridal show, my car was hit by an 18-wheeler truck. Skidding in the rain, projected over the highway dividing wall, my car was then plastered by a bobtail truck on the other side, with my trunk going through the windshield. It was the first day I had worn my seat belt! My neck, back, and rib bones were broken and twisted. I quit breathing and my heart stopped four times over three days. Some paralysis, wheelchair, and major physical therapy until I was thirty. Dance, my stress outlet, was over.

I would lose more battles in this hidden war of red – relative, stranger, date, colleague, handyman, driveway rape. I seemed to be a magnet for sexual assault. It was like there was a target on my back and I kept being in the wrong place at the wrong time. We all have things that happen in life that we don't understand. For me, that would be betrayal and sexual traumas. I was thirty years old the first time I said the word "rape." Each taking of my body and soul was different, yet they were all the same. Targeted, manipulated, violated, victimized, abused, blamed, shamed, silenced. A pattern. It seemed to be in the air I breathed.

Later, at my first engineering job, I was excited about another work party, but nervous that my presence as manager would change the atmosphere and people would put filters on because I'm there. I straightened my red pinstripe pantsuit and go in. Smiles. Say hello. See who's all here. We all are. Someone asks me, "Are you ready for a drink?" I certainly could use some perking up from that coffee after another long-ass workaholic week. I sip the coffee from a white cup. I was standing in the kitchen. The kitchen cabinets are white. More people, strangers from a nearby bar, came in. It was so crowded. Then I was in a lounge chair in the living room. Then I was awake. No one is here. No one is anywhere. What? I am in a man's blue denim shirt and my underwear. There is nothing in this room but a mattress. My shoes and keys are neatly placed on the wood floor. But no red pantsuit. I walk around calling for help. I feel the earth rotating and spiraling. I walked outside and there was my car. I get in. I do not remember driving home. Everything is black.

Then the phone rang and rang. It was my boss. He yelled, "It is Wednesday now! We don't have time for this!" I did not know what I said. I felt hollow. I was thinking about the bathroom. Then everything went black. Another time I was on the phone and a friend kept talking and talking. Why is he so excited? Why is he so worried? Why is he leaving his new dream job to come home from Europe? And why don't I just let him? Why am I so tired and wobbly? I can't think. I can't do anything. I didn't know what I was doing. I know I'm home, but I can't remember why. I don't even know if I should be doing anything. I didn't know what was happening. In the midnight hour, I awoke. Haunting scenes flooded my mind, but I could not truly connect. I saw different men's faces laughing, grunting, conquering me in a smoky red haze. It was stifling me, and I could not breathe. The stench permeated the invisible walls of my mind, penetrated the bounds of my body. I could not deny it. I saw red, followed by that familiar long trail of bloody images. I screamed and noticed my nest-bed I had been splayed out in with this sickness was drenched in blood, sweat, and a deluge of tears. I went back to work on Thursday. The fever was high, and I wondered what happened. What happened to everyone? What happened to my red pantsuit? It just disappeared like my memories. No one said anything as if nothing strange happened. Back to business. Back to managing. Back to being boss. Back to acting like nothing ever happened. I was really, really, *really* good at that now. I lived in silent shame wondering what do they know that I don't know? In my business suit, my nerves were shot. It appeared to me that I never told anyone how I found myself clothed. I also never said anything about the other room of video equipment and cameras. I couldn't believe or even contemplate that I was ever in that room. I would've remembered it, wouldn't I have? Yet this was not the house that the party was at either. I woke up in a different house entirely. How crazy was this? Believing no one knew anything, I soon started feeling at ease and peaceful. Good, no company ink was spilled in that red-stained purse. Danger averted. Except then my red pantsuit showed up at the front desk of the company, dry-cleaned, paid for in cash by a woman! My friend decided to call the police (without my consent). It all became public, and the case went to the FBI. I discovered I was drugged with a ten-cent date rape drug. The FBI questioned everyone. Everyone at work started avoiding me like the plague out of fear, and no one would speak. I admit I cannot fault them for it. It was scary for me too. I lost all my friends and coworkers over this. I left the company as fast as I could, giving up my chance for a promotion. I lost everything and everyone and I had to start over again. At age thirty, I quit wearing red.

After another broken engagement from a four-month whirlwind romance, a rough pregnancy and birth, I became a single mother of a tiny premature daughter. She cried in distress like a little bird that fit in the palms of my hands. Her father elected to return overseas right away. I was solely in charge of keeping another human alive. My dark history was forgotten in the distraction. I also got new shames, apparently as the only unwed mother in the day care system, and I was coughing for a year, so much that my coworkers complained to management. I was so busy, especially working in engineering that "IT" was buried. My coping mechanisms would continue to be workaholism, people pleasing, and survival mode.

At that point, the two girls of my psyche merged into one. I felt integrated and thought of myself as one person again finally. That defective and disgusting girl had just vanished into thin air. Maybe she was just finally shoved under that shag trauma carpet for good? By then I was thirty-four and my disastrous life was written all over my body. While devastated over the loss of another man and father for my daughter, I fought stage four sinus polyps and tuberculosis, a serious lung disease. I felt like life had either knocked the breath out of me or was suffocating me or both. The lungs are emotionally connected to sadness. I started to learn how my life was, how trauma was truly writing the story on my physical body. It made sense that I had a shameful sexual disease. It was no coincidence a 3.5 cm jaw tumor grew after being gang raped. I was never so silenced and locked up tight in my life. I started exploring the body, mind, spirit connection, and holistic alternative healing, but my laser focus was my daughter and my work.

Seeking healing and help, I did Pathways, a Dr. Phil type of boot camp coming out with a contract and covenant: "I am a Strong, Courageous Woman; Worthy and Trusting in God and His Love." While learning to embrace my contract and covenant, I was going into medical crisis after crisis, enduring several seizures and near-death experiences, and picking unavailable partners. It didn't matter that I'm a woman, physically or emotionally. These men weren't available to me. Subconsciously and unawake, I chose partners like my parents. I would pick partners, jobs, perhaps even a lifestyle, as well as coping mechanisms that would reflect my unhealed wounds from childhood including all those sexual traumas that I thought the deplorable girl took away with her. The family tree patterns would somehow repeat. When you and your body are treated like trash for extended periods of time, you begin to believe that is your worth. There's rape of your entire being and all that you are and all that you have.

In my late thirties, I got married, and through the fertility process and another difficult pregnancy and birth, I had a son. I also had eye socket surgery and chemotherapy to remove a growth blocking my eyesight. I still couldn't see the truth of how all this past trauma was impacting me. In hindsight, I think my body was trying to wake me up to that truth. We soon divorced and I became a single mother of two.

Four years later, now in my mid-forties, I married a codependent, emotionally unavailable, passive aggressive, and financially destitute man who was handsome, charming, soft-spoken, well-liked, and seemingly adored by others. I would learn this love was fleeting after I gave up my home, moved out of my home state, and signed the marriage document. From day one he withheld affection. On the second day, in the middle of the afternoon, my children and I found him using pornography in our living room. On day three I considered annulling the marriage but had hope things would get better. Less than two months later, in couple's counseling it was revealed he married me while infatuated with and lusting over a young French co-worker he kept waxing about. I was confused. I felt crushed. Like him, I began to blame my appearance and weight, though I wasn't overweight. I started to call myself the "it wife," a wife defective in womanhood in a non-marriage, a marriage on paper only. The next year we lost new friends over his dalliance, and he re-committed to our family. After he was let go from that job, I supported the family for two years while he was unemployed. I also helped fund his dreams of becoming a project manager, a drone pilot, a private pilot, and a commercial pilot. He promised to pay me back after he secured an aerial job. He promised a better future for us. He got that prized aerial job, but it required him to travel most of the year. After disappearing for days in Las Vegas, surfacing on the phone laughing in a car with another young girl he met, I decided the marriage was over. When he came back home, I ultimately forgave him, not wanting another failed relationship. I still had hope, though I was starting to misuse hope. He would continue to drain from my life savings, child support, and children's college funds by leaving us with little to no money from his earnings to pay bills. He donated to others for show while nickel-and-diming his family. I realized at some point that he was mostly affectionate in front of his family or when we were in church, loving and kind only when it suited his image. On his business trips, he would neglect, disappear, and abandon me and the children for days, weeks, and months. He would discard us randomly from overseas by email and texts before birthdays, Christmas Eve, New Year's Eve, days after my ministroke, and more. He would say the marriage was over repeatedly only to fly home and act as if nothing had happened, expecting a welcome home party and for life to revolve around him. From one of his last business trips, he allowed and supported another co-worker mistress to publicly humiliate and taunt me and my family on social media. She also posted herself wearing my clothes and other gifts that he gave her. After living a double life, this self-focused, self-important, and self-serving boy would leave me and my children worse off than how he found us. I would discover after a background check and pulling data off the computer that he lied and cheated while we were dating, engaged, and the entire marriage with multiple girls, fooling both our families, neighbors, and friends for over a decade. I had married a wolf in sheep's clothing of another kind. I finally confronted him with evidence of his cheating and soon after I was promptly devalued and dismissed, again by text. There was no apology. It seemed I had just been his financial rescue, a bank, and when my money was gone, so was he. He would under-employ himself during our divorce to manipulate spousal support. He had used well-honed covert narcissistic tactics of love-bombing, future-faking, pathological lying, stonewalling, twisting reality by gaslighting, triangulation, silent treatments and ghosting, hoovering, re-writing history, blame-shifting to avoid accountability and play the victim, word salad of circular conversations with nothing resolved, creating cognitive dissonance in me to avoid responsibility, stealing and damaging property, withholding love and affection all the while setting me up as "crazy" with smear-campaigns. I realized the stories I was told of his "crazy ex" before me, wasn't "crazy" at all. I was now labeled his "crazy ex." In my pain, I was emotionally reactive, depressed, and scared of what all this meant for my and my children's future.

Meanwhile, publicly portraying compassion, honor, and integrity, privately he had no empathy, no conscience, and no remorse. It was as if he was two different people. Like the hungry wolf, my once beloved husband had stalked into my world, and I found my life had been slowly and stealthily dismantled because I had chosen to dance with this charming villain and his dark side. After being harshly disposed of multiple times over the internet, I realized that the energy of rape can come by email and texts too. I learned there are all kinds of rape – visual, body, home, finances, dignity, time, sanity, and soul. It's an energy that manifests in different details, but the predator takes its prey in whatever way it wants. I learned that unconditional love is not unconditional tolerance. My unconditional love didn't conquer all, like I truly believed it would. This non-marriage showed me I needed to redefine love, change my ways of showing up in the world, reclaim my inner strength, and start over. I realized rebooting my life was becoming a skill, a necessary superpower, and easier each time. Later, after becoming very ill again from all this stress, losing my family home, and in fear of my life, I moved out of state before the divorce was final. I felt so shattered and broken, and like I had found my rock bottom or so I thought.

Rock bottom was the place where it felt things couldn't get any worse. My lowest rock bottom occurred when I completely dissociated. I detached from my body and my environment. I watched myself from the void above my body, unable to speak my truth like a normal human being. On the phone with that "golden-hair" boyfriend from my youth, I was shaking like a leaf in the winds of nervous meltdown, brain fog, and confusion. I was unable to speak my truth. I couldn't share what had happened in my life, nor what it was teaching me. I felt ashamed of my life. It was devastating. I felt like a failure. On that phone I was trapped in the silence of shame. Unfortunately, the "golden-hair" boyfriend of my youth had witnessed me in my brokenness. I knew then I needed to break out of that shelter of my comfort zone of silence and invisibility and accelerate my healing. This was a new low to start to rebuild my sanity and my life from out of the darkness and into the light. Rock bottom was the solid foundation I used to build the solid part of me from. I started to do new things to feel better. I dove into crocheting, studying metaphysics, and mastering Reiki to move my unhealed energy out of my being. Soon I had a major seizure that left me unable to speak for two weeks. I lost my hearing and my eyesight for two days. My muscles were twitching and spasming. I was in a wheelchair again for the fourth time in my life. My body was going down, it was all catching up to me. I felt broken, again. While I was still married and dancing through darkness of another kind, I attended Tiospaye, a self-development and emotional intelligence program. There my contract was "I am a powerful, beautiful, loving healer." I realized I needed to start living that contract. Also, I found Quora, another lifesaver healing arena, to learn about narcissism and post-traumatic stress disorder (PTSD). I started saving the writings that helped me in spaces called "Pathway to Peace" and "Broken Bird Mends." The Tiospaye program and the Quora blog engine, where I can read and write and receive support, helped expedite a return to balance and security. Mentally, I continued counselling. I continued working on my failing health. I was on oxygen for years, cancer was back, neurological issues were back. I couldn't breathe, my bones were rotting, and I was clumsy and couldn't move. Trauma was eating me alive yet keeping me stuck in a life I didn't want to live.

Trauma is defined as a non-daily occurrence or event that is a threshold moment; one over which we have no control. It's an "awakening point," a point that breaks you open; the opening that leads you to your very soul. It has a way of awakening us to a deeper level of viewing ourselves and our lives.

Trauma is the catalyst to "turn inward," to reprogram your inner belief systems that are no longer working for you. It's the conflict and fear that bring the chaos of change. Through the chaos, pain and suffering is what shakes your core and tears you apart. This is an opportunity to get down to the basics and put yourself and practically everything in your life back together. A return to your authentic truth, your true self. A return to innocence.

Trauma "motivates" us to find out who we are, what our values are, what we truly believe, what we can and cannot accept from ourselves and from others, what we are made of and how we want to live. We've got patterns to unlearn, wounds to heal, new ways of being in the world to embody. It's a steppingstone to our wisdom, to our natural gifts, and to our being beyond pressure, beyond all adversity.

On this path to freedom from trauma, there are some truths we may need someone to tell us if no one has yet. These truths I learned to live by to move forward:

- I am lovable. I am important. I do matter. This does not have to be a life sentence. Our life is not ruined. Our life is not a mistake to be erased. Suicide is not a valid solution. Do not give up. This suffering is temporary. Past traumas don't need to dictate the future.

- I am not my body. I am a soul in a physical body having a human experience on planet earth. Once I realized that I wasn't just my body, I quit blaming and detesting my body. Plus, every seven years, every cell in our body is regenerated. Thus, in seven years we will have a body that was never touched by the abuser(s).

- Sexual assault is not the victim's fault, and we didn't ask for it in any way. No means no. Silence, being unable to speak, doesn't mean yes either for whatever reason - from psychotic break, unable to hold boundaries, drunk as a skunk, high as a kite, drugged up with hairspray, frozen with fear, whatever the case. Silence does not default to yes. The way we were dressed is irrelevant. No clothing item, even if provocative, says yes. The only yes is yes - unless you were underage and/or manipulated. If you said yes and were under eighteen, that is not yes for you were not equipped to manage this adult situation. You were manipulated and groomed into that yes and bear no responsibility for this. If you were over eighteen and in hindsight recognize you were manipulated and groomed into your yes, consider this was a learning experience. Consider that you will now recognize manipulation and will choose differently next time. We did the best we could with what we had at the time.

- Sexual trauma is not who I am. This is not my identity. We are not what happened to us. It's predator shame, not ours. We are not disgusting, dirty, damaged, less than, inadequate, unlovable, unworthy, broken, or defective. We are just in need of deep understanding, tender care, and healing love. We will move through this. We were victimized, but we are no longer a victim. We will become who we choose to be.

- It is okay and understandable if we love or have feelings for our perpetrator(s). We can become trauma bonded with them. This is common and nothing to be ashamed of. It's also okay to cut toxic people completely out of our life, even if it's a parent or sibling wanting to make amends. We are not required to be tied to anyone, not even by blood. We have the right to choose who we let into our circles of life.

- No one is coming to save us. We must find it in ourselves to do that. No one can do it for us. The only way out is through. It's an excruciating process. We can't make it go away but we can get through mental confusion, emotional lows, inner turmoil, and environmental upheavals and stressors. We must heal our own hearts. We get to ignite our own light and shine it however we want to. Start seeing yourself as who you really are right now. If you have survived sexual trauma, abuse, manipulations, violations, victimizations, and you are breathing, then you are your hero, your warrior, your rescuer. You hold space in the field of honor and valor. If you start longing for a rescue, remember who you are. You are the rescue mission.

- Not everyone may believe us. Not even our own family. They may judge us or even blame us. Even the doctor called me a tramp after the HPV lab results arrived. This is judgment. This is them. Not me. Not you. We don't have to prove anything to anyone. We don't have to explain. We don't have to spend time and energy on their refusal to listen and understand us. We don't need their validation and they aren't offering any real support. We don't have to share the details of anything with anyone, even if they demand to know. We have a boundary now for that. We have the right to privacy.

- People expected me to get over it in their timing, in their judgment. Know that we will get over it at our own pace. Trauma like this doesn't heal with only time. These are the folks who typically have no frame of reference for what we have endured. I am more understanding of them and their viewpoint now. Before it would exasperate me and trigger me to feel even more defective. I learned these weren't the people to walk with me through my healing.

- We need a support system. This isn't the time to go it alone. One immediate goal is to find that "Rainbow in the Dark" friend. Someone to vent and cry to that will listen without judgment but with compassion. Feeling heard and seen lets us know that we matter to another person. This is for our healing. It's also healing for us to hear ourselves speak about it. For hearing it out loud may reveal the gravity of the facts and this keeps us out of denial. Get a counselor or join a local women's support group. Find a church or equivalent group for spiritual nourishment. I attend a spiritual college that teaches me to work with my intuition, my energy. And my angels. I'm never alone when I awakened to angel help and spiritual guidance. I attend Wayshowers College and Peace Community Church, International to teach me how to use my God-given spiritual gifts and connect with angelic counsel.

- The real battle was with my own feelings. This may be the toughest journey we'll face. This encouraged me to observe my thoughts, identify my patterns, commit to transforming my thinking and take full responsibility for my emotional health. Patterns and triggers stimulate past pain and are reactions when we are confused and out of coping mechanisms. Anger outbursts cover the intense emotions of fear, pain, and frustration. These behaviors are projected onto us from the perpetrators. We can and often do pick up their behaviors. Whether it's as predator or prey. This energy is also absorbed in our programming, especially in childhood. This explains how so much of this is multi-generational. Grandfather to father to son. Grandmother to mother to daughter. Or any mix of gender or family members. Triggers point us to where we are unhealed. Triggers in that sense, are good pointers toward healing ourselves. A trigger is a reminder of something we don't want. This is an opportunity to feel and heal, to clear patterns in our life and potentially in our children's lifetimes going forward. We can learn to respond to others instead of reacting to them.

- Left unhealed, there can be hidden impacts of trauma. I lowered my standards for what I would tolerate. I became a people-pleaser and over-gave my resources, especially time and money, to ensure I would be valued, safe, and loved. I abandoned my dreams to support the dreams of others. Out of fear, I picked partners that were unavailable or wouldn't touch me. I was still living in victimhood and unhealed.

After feeling victimized, we need the ability to recover ourselves. The good news is that trauma can be healed through the recovery process, consciously taking steps to heal the wounds and after-effects of it. The world the way we know it has changed. Trauma changed our personal truth, our inner world. Recovery from sexual trauma is about how to consciously heal the after-wrath of it, reclaim and rebuild personal truth and live authentically. It's about reclaiming our convictions and standards - and doing things we really don't want to initially do; things requiring us to change. To come out of any comfort zones that aren't for our highest good, coping mechanisms and addictions may need to be stopped. Trauma bonds and relationships may need to end, fears may need to be faced, inner thoughts may need to be transformed to reflect healthy self-love and consideration. Toxicity in all forms requires detoxifying actions, which may be hard. There are no shortcuts. We must do the work to move through it. "Personal truth" is what you really believe about who you are. It's not how you present yourself at work. Not how you present yourself as a parent. Not how you present yourself out in public. We all have one. Our personal truth is so important because we generate the results in this life that we believe we deserve. It determines how we treat ourselves, how we express ourselves, how we manage relationships, how we parent, how we handle money, how we operate in the world. It's the lens we see everything from. Now, the lens we look at life through has changed, skewed by things beyond our control. It's our personal truth that must be restored when we are in pain and suffering or numbed.

Another aide to recovery, self-love is honoring, respecting, and caring for our well-being. It's attending to ourselves first. On an airplane, we put our oxygen mask on first so that we are then able to assist others with theirs. We must tend to our needs first or, frankly, we could be a burden to others. Self-love is about being our own partner at times. Your relationship with yourself is so important because in your lifetime, you are the only one you will never lose. When we can love ourselves in a healthy manner, this is not selfish, it's "soulfish." Self-care is not selfish. Programmed to believe self-love and self-care was selfish, I coined this term "soulfish" so I could learn how to make myself a healthy priority in my own life without feeling guilty about it. My autonomous self could matter without being selfish. I could be kind and loyal to self, quit worrying about others, quit making others' needs more important than mine. Ask, "What do I want? What am I working toward? Is this good for me? What outcome would I like?" Self-love is about starring in our own lives or someone else will. What is inside us is the gold, our inner sun. Just care for your soul like it is the treasure of your lifetime. The truth is that it *is* the treasure. As you are remembering that you start to value yourself. We are healing from the inside out. Be considerate, honest, and loving with self.

Self-love is also about accepting our body as a temple. We must accept our body because it is a part of our essence. It is the vehicle for our soul. Start with your toes and go up. Begin to look at yourself in the mirror with full acceptance of your body and say, "I love you" and mean it. Self-love is also about listening to our body. Our body hears everything. It hears what we say and what we allow in our world. It absorbs and responds to everything. Our body is a measure, a tool. It can help us to discern what is for our best good or what pathway will generate the best outcome. It can help us to detect what or who to avoid as well. Our body is a great compass and guidance system. Ask, "How does my body feel? Am I collapsed into myself? Is an organ asking for attention?" Self-love is carving time out for our self-care. Self-love is setting personal boundaries and being able to say "No" to others, without guilt or shame. Boundaries are the mental, emotional, and physical fences we create to protect ourselves from being used, manipulated, or violated by others. A lack of boundaries invites a lack of respect and being taken advantage of. True self-love is our ability to manage ourselves when others are pushing our boundaries and life isn't so easy. "Soulfish" is the healthy act of self-care and self-love. Being "soulfish" is not selfish. We can lose the ability to care for and look after ourselves. Make lists and set alarms on the phone until self-care becomes a habit. Get back to the basics of building a routine. Because of our brain on trauma, we can get to the end of the day without having eaten, showered, worked, self-cared or self-loved. Be conscious, though, of overindulging in self-love and self-care to the point that opportunities are missed, that obligations and commitments we made become broken promises, and our integrity is lost. Balance is key. Refrain from developing unhealthy coping mechanisms like cutting, pulling out hair, drinking, smoking, drugs, workaholism, overeating, gambling, self-beating, overspending, ruminating thoughts of suicide, and more. We need to be mindful of the fact we are vulnerable to choosing self-destructive habits to numb our pain. It's important that we take time to do healthy things we love.

When experiencing highs and lows in life, smiles and tears, you'll have the experience of fear - viscerally. Like fears of relationships ending, jobs ending, and even the fear of success. These limiting beliefs are the core things and concepts that need to be upended. The divine purpose of fear is to move us through our comfort zones. While that can be scarifying, when we face fear with bravery and courage, we will realize that it wasn't as big as we thought. When we walk through our fear, our fire, to the other side, to that place where we did it and where we accomplished something, we gain confidence, inner security, inner authority, and most importantly we take our power back. Look, we did it. When we persevere through our fear, we build resilience and soul stamina. When we conquer that fear, when we feel that victory we are learning to blast through all adversity. Fear has a good quality of keeping us moving forward and growing.

The more pieces of myself that fall into place, the more I master my mood, my perception, and my responses and actions.

To master ourselves has a lot to do with mastering our thoughts and our emotions, especially the pain. Pain breaks us apart before it becomes beautiful. Pain transforms us into a soldier, into a warrior. Tackle the emotional madness. Pain tames our sensitive heart and makes it tougher to withstand the battles of grief and loss. With renewed strength, we reclaim our power. We can do this! Emotions are part of our survival, though challenging and difficult at times. Sometimes they are suppressed and repressed. We can't clear emotions we can't feel. Feel that pain from the past. Drop into your heart and feel all the feelings that are in your heart, for all time. Maybe you are reminded of childhood or a dream of the distant past, in another time, another place. Just feel, don't escape, or get distracted. Sit with the feelings as they come up. Cry for months if you need to. These are tears, well-shed. Scream if you need to. These are words, well-said. This process is where the healing lies. Trust the process. Anger may be telling us where we feel powerless. Anxiety may be telling us where our life is off balance. Fear may be telling us where we feel vulnerable. Apathy may be showing us where we're overextended and burnt out. Grief may be showing us what we love and care about. Unpleasant feelings aren't random, they're messengers, even alarms. Let the pain speak to you so you can release it. We can express our emotions by using our voice, taking a stand, writing, singing, screaming, painting, sculpting, dancing, doing breathwork, whatever works. It starts with us. Be willing to love yourself enough to meet your wounds and release them. Ask, "How does that make me feel? What do I really want? How bad do I want it? What would I need to change for that? What is stopping me?" Use this pain as a motive to take a step forward every day to make a change. Don't let the pain of the past consume us today. Beating ourselves up needs to stop for our mental and emotional health, and ultimately, our physical health.

We can take responsibility for our thoughts and feelings. We can be accountable for how we are feeling, what we are thinking, and what choices of actions we are making. We are responsible for those consequences. Remember, inaction is an action. Responsibly, we can act. We can learn to *respond* as opposed to *react*. The thoughts we choose to think are the tools we use to paint the canvas of our lives. Because of this, in a sense, our tomorrow is in our hands today. Think thoughtfully. I discipline and heal my thoughts stabilizing my mind. I say "Cancel, Clear, and Delete" to cancel any effects of my lower thoughts manifesting in my world. I replace the thought with a positive thought or word. This teaches me to discipline my thoughts, as well as uplift them into the positive. I also use "Soul Affirmations."

Soul Affirmations are self-talk tools that transform your inner world, moving you from painful belief systems and thoughts to peaceful thoughts and authentic belief systems. They are positive reinforcing messages that we give to ourselves, to reprogram our old beliefs about ourselves and to reassure our "inner child" that we are going to take care of her. They are powerful tools to transform our inner thought life and to create new neural pathways. They replace painful thoughts with peaceful thoughts. Feel yourself shift from feeling pain into feeling more peace. Write them out on your mirror with eyeliner for fun and repetition. Many put reminder notes all around their space. Repetition is important to build new neural pathways and overwrite the automatic negative tapes running in your conscious and subconscious brain.

Examples of Soul Affirmations:

- "I give myself permission to exist."
  (Reclaim your footprints and "sense of self.")
- "I accept myself as I am."
- "*YourName*, I am willing to learn to love you."
- "*YourName,* I love you."

45

- "I can do this!"
- "I am determined to do whatever it takes to move me forward."
- "I am the master of my energy. I am the master of my life."
- "I make my own goals and crush them."
- "I am at peace with my past."
- "I have a new zest for life."
- "I am a magnet for joyful experiences."
- "Everything is always working out for me."
- "I take time for myself."
- "I love my body, I listen to my body, and I take care of my body."
- "My body operates effectively and efficiently."
- "I am beautiful inside and out."
- "I feel great. I feel happy. I feel joyful."
- "Every day in every way, I am getting better and better."
- "I speak with strong confidence."
- "I totally forgive myself and others in my life."
- "I am grateful to everyone in my life."
- "Men always treat me well."
- "It is safe to feel my fear."
  (To assist you in the moment of panic attack or trigger.)
- "It is safe to be here."
  (Rub fingers up and down arms. Practice feeling safe.)
- "You have no power over me."
  (Say for predators, cravings, unwanted thoughts and emotions, others' opinions.)
- "I reclaim my power, my rights, my voice."
- "I am okay. I am safe. I am loved."
- "I am free! I am free!! I am free!!!"

Lastly, a good concept to master is forgiveness. Without forgiveness, we will live with powerful acid in our souls. Emotional pain will keep us in chains and tied to the perpetrator and those events, while we continue to suffer. Forgiveness does not mean condoning the behavior or the act. It means we cut the cord to it, detach from it, and release it. The more we release it, the more joy will naturally come to us. When I forgave myself for all the times that I thought I wasn't good enough, smart enough, or worthy enough, I then didn't feel like I had to prove myself or explain anything to anyone. I was able to not take things so personally. To heal, I took full responsibility for all assaults and traumas. I no longer blamed others for any of it. It woke me up. To grow, I let all of it go. I reclaimed my body, my thoughts, my feelings, my truth, my power, my soul, my life. Used correctly, trauma is the catalyst to the life we want! When we set our mindset to be a student of whatever happens here on Planet Earth, the trauma story loses its grip, its emotional charge. It becomes neutral. This is forgiveness, and this is healing.

As we dance through brokenness, new versions of ourselves emerge. We have perseverance, resilience, and soul stamina. When pain transmutes to peace, we triumph over trauma! When we light ourselves up and dance out of the darkness, we move from victim to victor!

Those days in the mountains of my youth, carved the nether reaches of my heart and taught me how to dance through time. May the tears and rain never put my spark out but ignite new flames to carry me through the valleys and beyond to the next horizon. The welcoming of the unknown terrain I embrace because my life depends on finding the **path of victorship** after the decades of dancing through the darkness of trauma, abuse, and loss.

With love,
Deborah Evans

ABOUT THE AUTHOR: DEBORAH EVANS

Deborah Evans is a mother of two young adults, a patented software engineer, Usui and Holy Fire Reiki master, spiritual educator and consultant, galactic librarian, and contributing author for "Expressions" and "Spirit is Our River" magazines. She is passionate about using her life experiences of trauma and abuse to help individuals find their voices, overcome limiting beliefs, heal with love, and live life fully. She survives on coffee, Wordle, music, dancing, crocheting, wire-wrapping stones, strolling through enchanted forests, gazing at the stars, and exploring the Akashic records.

If you want to experience healing bytes and share your story, please visit her free Quora spaces: "Broken Bird Mends" and "Pathway to Peace."

THREE

THE SHATTERED HEART
by Tamara Faust

Break Down

July 2001

*G*od, please don't let me die! I want to see my little girl grow up. I had to protect her. As I lay in the hospital bed hooked up to numerous monitors and IVs, all I could think about was that God could not let me die. I was too young and didn't want my little girl to be raised by her father. I wanted to see her grow up, get married, and have babies of her own. Would I get that chance? I didn't know.

Earlier that day, I'd felt that familiar heart burn giving me trouble, and it just wasn't going away. Nothing was helping. I started feeling weak and knew I should get help. I called several members of my family…. no answer. Where was everyone? What good did it do to have a mobile phone if you never turned it on. I felt frustrated with underlying fear. I debated over and over about calling 911, worried I'd be wasting their time, and by the time I knew I didn't have a choice I was almost too shaky to dial the phone. Not a good sign. Soon the fire department and ambulance arrived at my door, although I was too weak to leave my bed. The paramedics said my pulse was that of a seventy-year-old, which is obviously not what a young healthy thirty-year-old woman should have. I was 110 pounds, solid muscle, and other than some allergies, I was in great health. When my sister arrived, the paramedics told her that I needed to go to the hospital.

While waiting for the tests results in the ER my ten-year-old daughter was brought in. As I watched all the color drain from her face, I thought she was going to pass out. I could see the waves of fear rolling off her as I had her climb in the bed with me, telling her that Mommy was going to be okay. Praying it was true. Please God don't let this be the last memory she has.

The doctors gave me antacid, which took away the pain in my chest. But when I asked about the pain radiating down my left arm, they had no answer and were not willing to look further into it. Instead, they released me to go home. My sister dropped me off at our parents' house, and I just laid down on their bed. Still no word from them and I felt so alone. Thankfully they arrived soon after that. As the day progressed, the pain wasn't letting up, so Mom and Dad took me back to the ER. Another round of tests. This time the doctor diagnosed me as having Pleurisy, which is swelling around the lungs or heart, and put me on a large dose of Ibuprofen then sent me home, again. It took a week for my strength to return so I could go back to work.

September 2001

I was staying at a friend's house in Albuquerque when the heartburn reared its ugly head. I fought with it all through the night, several times going to my friend's bedroom door, about to knock to and seek help. But that negative little voice inside my head would stop me. "It's just Acid Reflux," said that voice, "Remember last time? They sent you home and made you feel like you had wasted everyone's time". And I would turn and walk away. Early that morning I drove myself to the ER and went through the process of signing in, but once again I listened to that little voice of doubt. I was feeling better and left without seeing a doctor.

October 2001

It felt as if my sinus infection had slid down into my lungs. My chest hurt and the shortest walk would put me out of breath. I was put on a round of antibiotics. Six weeks went by with no improvement, and the doctors didn't have any answers. They tested me for asthma, but it showed up negative. The only thing that seemed to help clear up some of the breathing issues was a lung supplement called Pneumotrate from my Chiropractor.

March 2002

I met with a pulmonary specialist who ordered a methacholine challenge test, which is a type of bronchoprovocation test used to help diagnose asthma. Methacholine causes mild narrowing of the airways in the lungs after injecting the medication directly into my artery. When they tell you it will be numb and you won't feel a thing, they lie! Sure enough my levels of oxygen dropped the required percentage....because *I had asthma*. However, when they gave me Albuterol to open the airways again, it only brought me up to 90 percent and a second dose dropped me back to 80 percent. Turns out I was allergic to Albuterol, and unfortunately there really wasn't any other medication I could use. The doctors were satisfied they had their answers—asthma. I was then put on Prednisone and several other medications. These medicines then affected my thyroid, and I gained twenty pounds in one month. Not to mention the water retention. One by one I went off the medications and managed to lose the weight. Long term result is I have fought my weight ever since, which also affected my self-esteem.

Okay, so I had asthma. I could live with that. Even though my asthma wasn't like any of my friend's asthma. I simply became out of breath while they would wheeze for air. *The doctors are always right. Right?* The next fifteen years went okay physically – though I never stopped fighting the weight gain. I still had some heartburn and would get out of breath, but I wasn't about to let a little asthma slow me down. I had a daughter to raise and still loved being very active dancing, hiking, and riding horses. I went scuba diving in the Cayman Islands and back country skiing up Cumbres Pass in the San Juan Mountains at an elevation of 10,022. I was doing great. *Right?*

What I didn't acknowledge was the loneliness and depression that I kept buried. If I was busy enough, I wouldn't have to look at it or feel it. Sweep it under the rug, keep going, just keep going.... Work, hobbies, church, my daughter's activities—anything to avoid the spiral. While I didn't consciously admit the depression it showed up through the many poems and songs I wrote. In the depths of these soul revelations, I can see the notes of faded hope drowning in the words. "My Name is Fear", "When's It Gonna Be My Turn", "Silence" and many more.

Revelation

March 2010

I didn't have the energy to go on walks anymore. I would go to my car and take naps during breaks and lunch. And my heart would always race, taking a few minutes to settle down. I knew I should get it checked out, but there was so much going on. I broke my nose the past summer and the infections wouldn't go away. There was no relief from the sinus congestion and headaches. During my consultation with the ear, nose and throat doctor, we found my sphenoid, a compound bone that forms the base of the cranium, behind the eye and below the front part of the brain, was completely closed along with a deviated septum. We decided to have surgery to fix the issues. Drilling through the sphenoid would be a very dangerous undertaking, and if anything went wrong, I could end up with brain injuries or death. I was willing to take the risk and face death if it came to that. I figured I would get the heart pounding checked after the surgery.

The morning surgery went beautifully, however several hours after coming home the pain medication given me in the hospital started wearing off. I couldn't keep the prescription pain pills down. As the doctor's office closed at noon I couldn't get the prescription changed. The pain became so unbearable that my parents took me to the Emergency Room (ER). By the time I'd arrived, the pain had become excruciating. It hurt too much to even speak or move my head. I remember sitting in the wheelchair with a blanket over my head desperately trying to block all noise.

After what felt like hours, I was given medication through an IV that brought much needed relief, like going from the burning sun to gliding into a cool mountain lake..., the pain just sliding away. Saturday went well; however, trying to sleep upright that night, I didn't feel good. Nothing I could put my finger on or put into words.... just not *right*. I asked to go to Urgent Care, looking for confirmation that I was okay. Instead, that trip was the start of the downhill slide. At the Urgent Care Clinic my EKG was abnormal, so I was transferred by ambulance back to the hospital.

I was calm in the ER room, knowing I wasn't afraid of death even though I was only forty-four years old. My daughter was grown, attending college, and I knew my parents would be there for her. Another EKG, more wires, an Echocardiogram, and finally an Angiogram, followed by the hushed tones of the doctor as he explained that my right artery was completely blocked which had caused a massive heart attack, sometime in my past. The heart attack had damaged 45 percent of the heart. It was too late to put any stints in to open the artery. I was now a high-risk patient for another heart attack or stroke.

My heart had been compensating. Instead of making new arteries, which often happens when an artery is damaged, it took my existing left artery and tripled the size. The medical culprit being an extremely high level of LDL (bad) cholesterol with numbers around 370, normal is considered 129 or less. If you don't have enough HDL (good) cholesterol to offset the LDL's it can clog up your arteries. High LDLs can be passed down through your DNA. I had inherited the super-duper bad cholesterol gene from both parents. Thanks Mom and Dad! I still love you anyway.

After the revelation of the now "heart issue", depression would become a continual companion for years. Sometimes I was able to fight back or ignore it by being "busy". Other times I wondered why I bothered to continue living. Then I would struggle out of the darkness to keep hope alive. Each passing year become harder to get through. The loneliness, financial struggles, and what felt like never-ending obstacles were faced alone. The holidays were challenging, but especially Christmas. As much I loved the lights, music, giving of gifts and honoring Jesus birth, was the most difficult. Thirty years of Christmas without someone special in my life, to share the burdens, laugh, to be held and loved. As I think about the past I allow my mind to drift back….. to all the ones who contributed to my broken heart and played a major role in helping me become who I am today.

Betrayal and Rejection

1980

It all started as a very young teenager when I met the Player. He was handsome and charming. I was so shy and naïve, but his personality tugged at me. He knew his wild and rowdy ways would not fit my innocence—something I wouldn't realize for many years to come. All through high school, we circled the pull of attraction, and upon graduating, he left to follow his dreams of being a professional bull rider.

Everything in me says run. Cause baby you're a loaded gun.

January 1984

When I started college, along came the Puppet Master. Dark hair, beautiful brown eyes, and pretty boy handsome. I had decided that he was the "One" by the end of our first date. In those first months of dating, we'd sit in his truck and he would just listen to me talk. Finally, someone who was interested in hearing what I had to say and before long I made him my whole world. His puppetry started out slowly. Telling me if I would talk a certain way more people would be interested in what I had to say. I should wear more makeup. "Oh look, some lovely clothes I picked out for you". I didn't realize that I wasn't good enough just being me. This was the start of eroding my self-confidence.

The dresses he chose shouted sex, short and form-fitting, the tops belly-baring. Shortly after I had turned twenty-one, we went to the bar to go dance. He had me wear a short, red spandex dress off the shoulders, with high heels. We were sitting at a table near the dance floor, when he got up and left me there alone saying he'd be gone for just a minute. I felt very self-conscious in the outfit, my first time being in a bar, and just plain insecure. Men would come up and ask me to dance, which I refused all the while looking around for my boyfriend. Where was he? Later, I learned that he had gone up stairs, watching to see how many men hit on me. So became the Puppet Master. I was the doll to be dressed up and played to his whims, to be shown off as a trophy. Yes, in his own way he loved me, but it was more about him than me. I went along with all of this, burying any objections, and my voice became almost non-existent.

I worshiped the attention he gave me and was hurt when ignored, and somewhere inside me grew a belief that I wasn't good enough. We were the classic co-dependence relationship. I could fix him, and he needed to be in control, so we were like a Moth to a Flame.

January 1989

Eventually, we got married. I couldn't wait to take his last name and be "someone", a wife. We had our ups and downs as any couple does. The turning point was when unplanned, I became pregnant. I was thrilled and thought, finally, *someone who will love me unconditionally.* That thought alone should have been an a-ha moment, but it slid in and out with only a remnant remaining. I loved my growing baby, often singing to her as I traveled back and forth to work. My husband, not so thrilled to say the least. This baby was a burden that he wasn't ready for and the first words out of his mouth when I told him I was pregnant was to get an abortion. I refused, and my pregnancy became the elephant in the closet. I was nine months along and weighed 123 pounds, yet I was "fat" in his eyes.

January 1991

Once our beautiful little girl was born, he became a proud daddy, which meant showing her off, but not actually helping take care of her without an argument. This precious bundle of joy suffered from the turmoil in the house, yet her sunny disposition was a balm to my soul. The instant she woke up in the morning, you could hear her gurgling and blowing bubbles. Her smile would light up when she saw you. She was so beautiful with large brown eyes, long dark eyelashes, cute chubby checks, button nose and rose bud lips. A true joy and blessings that I'll forever be thankful to have.

While I adored my baby girl, the lack of sleep, physical and emotion neglect, and working full time took a toll on me. I became colder and colder to my husband, and our fights became worse. He always had a cutting tongue, and it grew even sharper. There were nights I curled up on the edge of the bed, him screaming obscenities and insults at me, even when I didn't respond. Each word cutting deep into my soul. The number of scars growing inside me, the kind that do the most damage, yet no can see. His anger was getting out of control. He would back me up against the wall and punch his fist beside my head. This was no longer a relationship, and the marriage was coming to an end. I was willing to put up with a lot for myself but I couldn't, wouldn't, raise my daughter to go through the verbal abuse I was experiencing. Seven months after giving birth I left and filed for divorce.

Dark Water
Oh black water why does my image appear on your smooth surface? Staring back at me through haunted eyes, bleak with despair. Release me from your dark, mysterious hold. Let me surface to the light I see above. I reach my hand up, but it never breaks through.

September 1992

At this point I didn't know who I was. I couldn't even tell you what type of clothes I liked because I hadn't picked out my own in years or without approval. As I was transitioning to finding me, enters the Alcoholic. Sweet, and shy, with a heart of gold. He was amazing with my daughter. After I signed my divorce papers, we moved in with him. I was attending college night classes, and when he got off work, he would stop at my mom's house to pick up the baby who was now a year old. When I came home, all her bottles were made, he had given her a bath and put her to bed. He'd also made dinner for me. He never complained about taking turns getting up in the night when she woke up crying. He loved her as if she were ours. We would be in different rooms working on hobbies or homework, and he would come find me just to give me a kiss then without saying a word go back to what he was doing. All of this was way beyond what I had ever experienced. I felt cherished and loved.

There was only one issue. He was an alcoholic. We talked about his alcoholism, and he started attending AA classes. I thought we were doing really well. We had been together for eight months. We were talking marriage, and I was ready to jump in with both feet. I asked if we could go out dancing for my birthday on the condition that he was okay with being around the alcohol. He said it wouldn't be a problem. That night, he snuck drinks behind my back and after a huge fight admitted to hiding liquor. All I could think about was him having drinks with the guys after work, then coming to pick up my daughter. It terrified me, and again we fought. The next day he hooked up his trailer and left without a word. Baby girl would stand at the fence looking out to where the trailer sat and call "dada". She was just as lost as I was. No goodbye, no chance to fix things—just gone. The men I met afterwards were always measured against the way he treated me. Most of them never even came close.

Was it a good thing he left? Maybe. I heard that several years later he married and had a little girl of his own. His wife threatened to leave if he didn't quit drinking. I guess the lesson was finally learned. They are still happily married today. I wish them both many, many more years of blessings.

1992

I was alone again and scared, my fears of the unknown became more intense than the familiarity of going back to what I knew.

Feeling like a failure, I figured if my ex-husband and I were happy once, then maybe we could be again. Conveniently pushing the reasons why I left in the first place to the back of my mind. We went down the path of reconciliation three times. First, we went to a Christian counselor who said we had a communication issue. Sure, verbal abuse is a communication issue I thought sarcastically. Yet in all honesty I also struggled to communicate effectively. Fear of speaking up for what I wanted and needed. Several more counselors and nothing changed. I still had no voice, nor did I understand how to use one to express what I needed, wanted, or my frustrations. Then, we went to Family Crisis and we each saw different counselors whose advice contradicted each other. He could have any friend he wanted including the ex-girlfriend who called multiple times. We were told to have date nights and nights out with our friends.

I did not believe we should be going to the bar without each other, and he thought differently. Most of the time when it was my turn to go out, I passed. He always took the Wednesday night ladies-get-in-free-at-the-Top Deck, and then would come home and tell me how many women tried to pick him up. He would dig the phone numbers out of his pockets. Driven by my own insecurity, I decided to take my night and go to a movie with a girlfriend. After I arrived home from work to get ready, he started a fight, accusing me of planning to go to the bar instead of a movie. By the time I walked out the door he was screaming at me, and I was in tears. I look back and realize the intent was to make sure I didn't have a good time. After the movie I was still very upset and hunted up a mutual friend. I was hoping he might have some answers as to why the Puppet Master would treat me this way. The friend didn't have any answers and I ended up crying on his shoulder. Pouring all the confusion, hurt and anger out in a river of tears.

I found a book called *The Verbally Abusive Relationship,* and it changed my actions. The counselors had all said I couldn't do anything about what he did and said but this book gave me tools and helped me to recognize manipulation tactics. The author warned that the partner will either appreciate it to help them overcome the anger issues or it would escalate the situation. Ours escalated. During one argument he gripped my arms and threw me on the bed. I had fingermark bruises the next day. I knew I couldn't continue this way. I felt like I had done everything possible to make the relationship work. Nothing was ever going to change and could potentially become much worse, because he had no desire to fix his issues. I walked away for good this time.

1995

One night after a rodeo in Belen, I became caught in the Player's web again. That night we started a lovers' dance that would last off and on for the next twenty-one years. He'd come to town with the circuit and end up staying with me for the night before heading down the road—for the next rodeo and next woman. I wasn't blind, I just didn't want to admit it to myself. I kept hoping he would finally see who I really was and choose me, instead of being left wondering what it would be like to actually date him.

1996

Ah now we come to the runner. I had met this man when we were younger, growing up in the same small town, but he was several years older than me and I really didn't know him. We met again one night when I was out dancing. We danced the night away and talked. The relationship progressed very quickly. I enjoyed having his company, and we both understood that we were "in love" with other people and that was okay. I was still hung up on the Player. He had been married twice before, and he was still in love with his first wife, the mother of his children. He moved in and we soon functioned as a family. My daughter adored him and they would often go hunting for bugs in the field or played games while I cooked supper. He became my best friend. I still had issues of trust and being too afraid to ask for what I wanted or address something that was bothering me. I wanted him to make it safe for me to talk about the issues. However, I was willing to work on it. As time went on, I found my fairytale dream with the Player became a true relationship with the Runner. We talked about a future together, and he said I could quit my job and go back to college full time. He would support us, even though neither one of us wanted to get married.

My heart and head filled with dreams of the life he painted. Several months into the relationship he was called to work in Las Vegas, NV. It would be long distance, but I felt we could make it work. It wasn't long before I could feel him growing further away with each phone call. He didn't have anything to do in the hotel room, so he would go to the bar in the evenings. This is what got him in trouble with his first wife. I went for a visit to Las Vegas, and he felt distant from me, continuing to pull away. When he changed phone numbers, he told me not to tell his first wife. No explanation, just an order. They had a child with an immune disorder which meant life or death at any time, and as a mother I felt it wrong to hide this information. A lot was playing in my head during this time. The looming possibility of him deciding he was done, fear of rejection again, anger at being ordered. Maybe I was out of line, maybe I wasn't. Maybe I was providing him with the excuse he was looking for or just a test to see if he'd stay. I called his ex-wife to give her the new number. Shortly after, he called and broke up with me. I lost my best friend, and my daughter lost another father figure. Our hearts broke all over again. Why wouldn't anyone fight to keep a relationship with me?

Is my heart half full of the love you gave or my
heart half empty, cause your love is gone.

1998

I told myself I was done and didn't want to meet anyone. I was just going to focus on my daughter and living life. One weekend I had a friend talk me into going dancing. My dance partner stopped a couple times to talk to one of the band members on stage. I never bothered to look up. I didn't care as long as the band could keep a beat, I just wanted to dance. When he stopped at the stage a third time I decided I was being rude and politely glanced up. The instant I met the Musicians gaze I was transported to another dimension. I literally could see into his soul and it was a mirror of mine. I saw his heart was ripped and torn, blood seeping out of the gashes. I stood in wonder, because here was someone who truly knew the pain I suffered. Then I realized he could see in me just as easily as I could him. My world went completely blank, losing all awareness of what was happening around me. When I did come aware of my surroundings, my dance partner and I were halfway around the dance floor and I had no idea how I had gotten there. I was terrified and furious that God put me in this position. I had worked so hard to piece my heart back together so many times, and now this man, this musician, could undo everything! My partner and I made several circles on the dance floor before I was able to calm down. I'd always had a strong faith in God and silently agreed to trust that God had my best interests in mind. As far as the Musician, I had no clue what he looked like, what he was wearing… absolutely nothing about him.

On break, my girlfriend couldn't wait for me to meet the band. I just wanted to run for the door. But since I couldn't come up with a good excuse to leave when I had just arrived, I sucked it up and prepared for the unknown. In meeting the Musician he held out his hand, which I reluctantly grasped. I was instantly calmed with peace washing through me. I'd never experienced anything like this and felt lost as to what I should do or think.

Over the next five years I went to see the band play and hang out as part of the group if it was out of town. I was confused as to how the Musician felt about me, but I didn't have the courage to ask. I felt, insecure, and shy, with the only way to speak to him was through letters. The letters were meant to give comfort, hope, encouragement, and allow him to see me, the person who couldn't speak when in his presence. We didn't talk about those letters, nor did he mention a girlfriend, but he didn't asked me to stop writing. He never wrote back and always accepted the small Christmas gifts with gratitude. Sometimes he would flirt with me, which I had no clue how to respond. There was a connection that neither one of us could explain. I hoped that it might someday lead to more. He, on the other hand, ran from it and kept me at a polite distance.

2001

The pinnacle came just before Christmas. I asked to speak with him, as I knew I couldn't keep giving of myself without much return on his part. I finally asked how he wanted me to treat him, and he said we would only be acquaintances. It was then did he mention the years of letters I had written. "Why didn't you say something?" I asked. "All you had to do was ask me to stop."

He stood in silence, searching for an answer that wouldn't come, before shrugging his shoulders with hands up saying, "I didn't want to hurt you.". "You're not." I replied. And in that *moment*, it was the truth. In an instant everything changed. The room filled with the presence of the Holy Spirit, an incredible energy force flowing into the crown of my head, out of my heart and straight at him. It was a pure unconditional love beyond anything I could have imagined. The force felt like a hurricane blowing through me and I remember wondering how he wasn't plastered against the wall behind him. As we stood looking at each other, he took a step closer, then another. Almost as if he was being drawn to me until a foot separated us. At that point his brother came to the door and the spell was broken. I was left standing in awe.

I have often wondered what would have happened had we not been interrupted that day. What was my purpose in that situation. I believe I simply was the vessel that God used to heal him of the emotional pain from broken relationships. What an honor to be chosen in that way. The experience opened up my eyes, and I wondered if I would ever be used in that manner again. I've often pondered what was it that he felt during that moment. I've seen him a few times over the years, yet never asked about that day. Later, as the emotional miracle faded, I found the relationship pattern of denied hopes for a future, and my heart was once again crushed.

The musician has been happily married for over 11 years to his 3rd wife. I wish them nothing but joy and love for the rest of their lives.

SILENCE

I have found it is not the words of rejection that
wound me so deep...as the silence.
The sound that has no sound.
It wraps me up in shadows and binds me
with silken threads
from which I cannot break free.
I am lost in a world that has no direction,
no beginning and no end.
The blade cuts swift and sharp with no escape.
My wounds weep with emotion,
but have no sound.
Words of healing I do not hear.
Is there no end to this torment......of silence.

Years went by as I had given up all hope of meeting someone who would treat me good. Someone who would stay, love me and fight for our relationship. Every time I met someone it was the same story over and over. I didn't want to continue that path so found it better to just not date. I didn't know how to break the pattern. Loneliness and depression became my sole companions. I filled my days and nights with activities to avoid their company.

> *Lonely days and lonely nights*
> *Don't want you in my life*
> *Lonely days and lonely nights*
> *I want you out of my sight*

September 2015

The Player called and wanted to see me. He was now a recovering alcoholic. I thought to myself, "Do I really want to go through this again?" Still, I needed closure one way or another— and I hadn't been on a date in more than ten years. I wanted to see if he had changed. It was familiar being with him, same ol' charmer, and I struggled not to get caught in the web again.

I learned many things about him that I didn't know. Years ago, he'd made a bet and set up a game with his brother of which I was the unknowing victim. We all lost the day he put it in motion. He decided to play a game of having me choose him or his brother for which I had no idea what was going on. There was no choice, as it had always been him. What I saw was him pushing me away again, triggering my greatest fear "rejection". I was deeply hurt but willing to leave the past in the past.

The Player kept in touch with me over the next couple months, and he visited me in December. I was finally being given the chance to see what dating him was like. A couple more months went by, and we agreed to meet up to listen to his cousins' band play out of town. Earlier that year I'd had knee surgery and was still on crutches. It was an unpleasant surprise when he invited his dance partner to come because he didn't know if I would be able to dance. We didn't have an exclusivity agreement, and I knew he was seeing other women as he was always *over eager* to share those details. He proceeded to flirt with his dance partner, telling me I had competition. While wrapping his arms around me and kissing my forehead. Even his cousins gave us questioning looks. What he didn't realize was I don't play the competition game. Not *interested*! As I was from out of town, we had made arrangements for me to stay at his house.

I'm sure your wondering *what in the world was I thinking and I should be kicking his ass to the curb!* I was trying hard to change my old patterns of flight and hide reactions instead of communication. What did I want out of this relationship? That night, he cuddled me all night, which felt like a warm cocoon I'd been missing for years. The comfort of just being held, giving the illusion of being loved. While I knew it was a lie, it was my turn to take something for me. I was no longer the silenced voice, and when I confronted him about his actions with the dance partner the next day, he admitted that he didn't realize that she was interested in him. He wanted to see where it might go with her.

Talk about feeling thrown away. It was the reality check I needed to see he had not changed, and this wasn't what I wanted. It took some time to get over the hurt and anger accumulated from over thirty years of rollercoaster dreams, hopes, and let downs. I couldn't meet his needs any more than he could meet mine. I understood and accepted we could be friends but not lovers. I finally closed the chapter of the Player for good. I wish him well and hope he realizes someday that everything he is seeking in a woman must first be healed within himself.

After two divorces he is still playing the field and throwing red flags out for anyone smart enough to look.

April 2016

I really wanted a relationship and was willing to start looking. While going through the process of closure with the Player, I connected with an old school mate through Facebook. The Facade was funny, thoughtful, and posted such beautiful sentimental sayings. *This must be who he was, right?* After several dates I thought, "Wow, where has this guy been hiding?". I was over the moon at the love being showered on me. He treated me just the way I had been looking for and seemed like the perfect catch. Keep in mind I'd been basically alone for close to 20 years. Within a month, he told me he loved me and talked of buying me an engagement ring. Two months in, at his urging, I was moved in with him. Shortly thereafter, things quickly deteriorated. He no longer cuddled me at night, sleeping with his back to me, and if I moved too close, he pushed me away. He also picked up smoking again and started drinking heavily. He didn't talk much and spent more time on Facebook.

One night he went for a ride on his motorcycle and didn't come back. I texted and called with no answer. What if something had happened, a wreck or worse? The next morning, I saw the post on Facebook. He was perfectly fine and had decided to go out of town. Not a word given to me. Filled with anger and hurt, I moved out. I was running away again. He didn't even notice I was gone until the day after he came home. I wasn't ready to give up on this *dream* relationship, so a week later we finally talked. He had PTSD from serving in the war and had gone off his medication, because "he was so happy with me".

If I wanted to stay with him, I needed to research PTSD to have a better understanding of it. He said it would take six weeks for the medication to start working again. Turns out it would take up to six months for the medication to work, not weeks. Meanwhile I dug in and started looking for answers. I found that most PTSD victims keep a very small circle around them, which would explain his lack of friends. I found group therapies and individual counseling with the VA and talked to other veterans to understand more. I read a great book called *Once a Warrior-- Always a Warrior* by Charles W. Hoge, MD, Colonel (Ret.). When I brought my findings to him, he was furious. Said he didn't have time for counseling and only needed his meds.

Ignoring the crimson red flags, I stayed patient, hoping the amazing guy would come back. Instead, I just got hurt—again and again. He was obsessed with other women's Facebook posts and hide text messages. The true narcissist was coming unmasked with games to be played. We attended a motorcycle rally where he left me at a table alone, while he snuck off to party with his ex-girlfriend. I found him flirting and having a great time, well on his way to being plastered. Later that night he tells me he loves me and wants to marry me. I wasn't sure I even wanted to be his girlfriend. It was a learning lesson for me that I was not willing to take care of a drunk!

Other instances happened, like when I had an allergic reaction to niacin that left my heart racing, but I didn't want to call an ambulance. Since he lived near the hospital, and I was scared to be alone, I called to ask if I could come over. He told me to just go to the ER and let him sleep. So I did just that. Later he said he had thought I wanted to make sure he didn't have another woman in his bed. I had never once accused him of cheating, so it must have been his guilt talking. I don't believe he ever cheated physically, but mentally and emotionally it was very prevalent. The drinking and lies became worse. He would go home and down six beers in thirty minutes, sometimes an entire twelve pack in a sitting. He confessed there were a few times he would become so drunk he had to call into sick to work the next morning. Had I known all of this, I would never have dated him. He would tell me on the phone, "I miss you, I love you, I want to marry you, but I don't want to see you. I like missing you, and you get on my nerves if I see you more than one day a week." In the end, he had no desire to work on himself, with my heart now *physically* in pain, I knew I couldn't sacrifice my health anymore.

I grieved over him for months and was angry for years. I cried for the dream of wanting to be loved and the loss of those dreams even if they weren't real. Once again, I had been fooled and betrayed. The pattern hadn't changed, just the name and face. I desired to be loved by a man so much that I was blind to how I was treated and put up with most anything.

There were a few others before and after the Façade, all showing the same symptoms of abuse, alcoholism, narcissism, and neglect. What was it going to take to break this pattern? Cut the ties of attraction, stop waiting for the guy that never got his act together, and heal the past so I might find a future? My search for the answers continued.

I've had a few male friends along the way that showed me there are men who can be trusted. They revealed pieces of what I want in a relationship. I'm so thankful to have these men in my life. Larry, who always has a joke, keeps me company for dinner and movies and listens to my hopeless love life. You encourage me to keep going. George…I'm so very grateful for this lifetime friendship. You've always been willing to offer a shoulder to cry on, stories of days gone by that keep me laughing, a place to stay when I was at rock bottom, and the companionship talks at the end of the day. I'm really glad you have that gorgeous woman at your side. After 30+ years, still hanging out with you. Todd, while our friendship is only seven years young you have become one of my best friends. The one I call when my world falls apart and you talk me through it. Who tells me "I'm so proud of you", and gives me a call on the first day of my new job to say "you've got this". The man that keeps me smiling and bubbling over with laughter. You've given me a safe place to find my voice even when I'm terrified to speak. The one that allows me to practice the skills I'm going to need to make a relationship work. Yeah, I'm a work in progress. You are always honest, even when it's not really what I want to hear and you don't get mad when I don't take your advice. Although they are really good suggestions. I look forward to many more years of "Tammy, I don't talk on the phone for 4 hours", but you do with me. I don't have the words to describe how very grateful I am for you Pal.

All the betrayals and pain of broken relationships have left me with a great distrust of men in general. Something else for me to work on. While I admit to sharing fault through co-dependent actions and lack of communication. I learned and grew from each relationship. Little by little putting boundaries in place for unacceptable behavior. Will the woman I am today put up with even a quarter of the crap I went through? No way! Do I believe those broken relationships and lack of hope contributed to my heart attack? Yes, absolutely. Our emotions can cause physical ailments.

The Search

I firmly believe that Western Medicine is necessary; however, Eastern Medicine and alternative medicines also have their place. As I would discover, there is more than the eye can see. I was a five-percent survivor, almost half my heart scarred, looking at a defibrillator and eventually a heart transplant down the road. By this time I'd been divorced for eighteen years with a string of broken relationships behind me. Sitting alone in my bedroom I completely broke down crying, thinking "No one will want someone with my condition. I'd just be a liability." All hope of finding a love that would treat me good was lost. Dreams and hope slid quietly away. I sat down and planned out my funeral, because obviously I didn't have a future anymore. It would take a while for me to realize if I'd survived this long without any medical help then maybe, just maybe, I could have the opportunity of a different outcome than what was predicted.

As a Christian I had read all the miracles in the bible and wondered why I couldn't have one that healed my heart, and thus began the search for my miracle. I read stories online and scripture. There were so many questions that ran through my head. "What did I do to deserve this? Was I not worthy? What would it take for me to be worthy?" At times I was very angry with God. I went to other churches with faith healers, and one time, there was a speaker who just held my hands, and I felt heat fill my heart for three days afterward. I thought surely this must have been answered prayer. Yet my EKG and Echograms hadn't changed. Even though I was disappointed, this gave me fuel to keep searching, and each step expanded my mind to more options than I had ever considered before.

During my path of finding answers, I started seeing a naturopathic doctor, named Christina, and to this day, I believe that she has been instrumental in saving my life many times. She was the one who had answers and offered good sound advice as to what I could do to control my cholesterol. She used muscle testing, a form of Kinesiology, to check for foods that were causing me inflammation. Of course, I had to be the one that needed to give up my delicious gluten-filled bread, corn, and dairy. Goodbye, my beloved Mexican food. I wasn't sure how I was going to survive without my go to comfort foods. With that said, when I followed my new diet, my weight slid off, and my LDLs dropped 100 points in one month. Not one of the many different medications I had tried accomplished that. Christina's help has allowed me to make a lot of progress towards healing. She is a God given gift for which I am eternally grateful.

I continued on my search for healing, my path lead me to "laying on of hands" by church healers, foot zoners, massage therapists, shamans, mystics, meditation tapes, intuitive healers, Reiki healers, tuning forks, vibrational MHz and those that used crystals or sound for healing. Each experience had a positive effect on me. My eyes were opened to see how God uses these people to bring healing to others.

During my journey of discovery in alternative healing, I've come to understand that most disease has an emotional base to it. When I took a good hard look at what was beneath the broken heart, it was depression, hurt, and anger. The loneliness of not having a man to wrap me in his arms, talk to me, allow me to lean on, and laugh with. The fear that I never would have someone special in my future, someone I could count on. The disappointment, that this was what life had to offer me. And there was anger and hurt at how I'd been treated by all those who had come before. The many years I'd spent crying over lost hopes. After all of that, I'd closed off my heart in order to protect it and stop feeling the hurt. Along the way I developed the belief that "I wasn't worthy to be loved."

Healer Is Awakened

June 2014

Thirty-year class reunion. In high school I had a good friend named Angie, but lost touch after graduation, however at our reunion, we reconnected over common interests in the healing modalities of foot zoning versus reflexology, detecting personality traits using graphology and exploring new spiritual paths. I was still searching for healing, physical and emotional as well as knowledge. She was far more advanced and soon became my mentor.

Angie suggested that I look up "chakras." Chakras are areas of energy in the body that run from the base of your spine to the top of your head. Admittedly, I didn't have a clue what a chakra was, so I bought *The Book of Chakras* by Ambika Wauters a beautiful, full-color book. It illustrates what each chakra represents, including the qualities, attributes, affirmations, and how each affects your emotions and physical body. The book provides meditations to open each energy center, so every day I went through the seven main chakras and practiced "opening" each one. Wow, the feeling of a *rush of energy* flowing up through my body and head was amazing.

Angie said to start feeling the vibration around me by using my own hands. The vibration can be similar to putting your hand on the hood of a running car. A large truck feels much different than a luxury car. I found everything had a vibration, whether it was plants, objects, food or people. I used the vibration while grocery shopping to test how fresh the fruit and vegetables were. A bouquet of flowers has become one of my favorite sensations. Each flower gives off a different vibration such as feeling waves of water washing back and forth on my palm, others have a cold breath of air, while another one spiky pricks. I still delight in the flower game. Keep in mind that each person feels the energy different. The way I relate to it does not mean you will also feel that same sensation. I found I really resonate with crystals and have filled my house with them. When the energy of a crystal pulls me in, I find it's what I need at that present moment.

Sound healing with singing bowls, drums and tuning forks is another form of healing that I've found to be very beneficial. It helps me to breathe more deeply and release negative emotions.

This led my curiosity to wonder about people and vibration. I had a friend who showed up with a stomach ulcer. My interest was piqued and she consented to let me see what I could feel. Agreeing that I wouldn't actually touch her. Within minutes of her closing her eyes she said, "I thought you weren't goin..." then stopped midsentence when she opened her eyes. Instead she said "It feels like your whole hand is laying on my stomach", yet my hand was 5 inches from her body. Now I was really confused but fascinated. What was that and why? When I asked my healer Christina, she said I was doing Reiki naturally and should become trained in it. Another new word that I had no clue what it meant.

Reiki

"Reiki (pronounced ray-key) is a Japanese technique for stress reduction and relaxation that also promotes healing. Reiki energy comes from an infinite source but is not tied to a religion.

Most Reiki healers or also known as Hands-On healing is given to a person through a Reiki attunement. An important point to note is that Reiki can never do harm. It is guided by spiritual consciousness and not the practitioner doing the healing but the loving presence of spiritual consciousness.

Life energy flows within our physical body through pathways called chakras, meridians, and can also be present and pass directly through the organs and tissues of the body. The free and balanced flow of healthy energy (Ki) keeps the body in good condition. When the flow of healthy Ki is disrupted, it causes diminished functioning within one or more of the organs and tissues of the physical body. This creates a blockage allowing disease to enter the body.

In a Reiki session, sometimes the person will feel a cold or hot sensation. The session is performed by the practitioner by first scanning the body for blocks, allowing spirit to guide them. They will then hoover their hands above the area or lay them directly on the person as per the receivers' comfort level. They will keep their hands there until spirit directs them to move. An average session lasts around an hour.

*All the information from **Reiki** *to* this point, is taken from (*Reiki The Healing Touch, First and Second Degree Manual* by William Lee Rand, Copy Right 1991, revised February 2016).

It is my firm belief that my attunement came straight from source on the night I had the conversation with the Musician. It lay dormant waiting on me to be ready. Reiki is not limited to just people but can be used on plants and animals. Animals often accept it much easier than people.

When working on someone my hands are always feeling a

variety of sensations. I find since my master certification in Holy Fire Reiki that they become extremely hot even if the receiver does not feel it. Along with the heat is the feeling of energy leaving my hands often lighting up my whole body. At times they are cold, the intensity so strong it is almost painful, soft ocean waves, or prickly as if they are waking up from numbness. I know I have so much learn. At this time I do healings and teach Holy Fire Reiki. I can't wait to continue my upward journey in this God given gift.

The healing I have received from others and the continual Reiki inside me has allowed me to change the course of my heart diagnosis. To this day I have no stints, no defibrillated and definitely not on a Heart transplant list. I will continue using numerous modalities of healers and my own Reiki until my spirit is safely tucked in her body, all blocks are gone and my heart is healed. The journey continues. I still have hope that there is someone out there meant to be my partner to love and walk life's pathways hand in hand.

I am a Reiki Angelic Master, certified Holy Fire III Master, and Holy Fire III Karuna Master. Please email me at Reikifirelight@gmail.com for a free list of the tools and books that have been an answered prayer in my life. My suggestion is to explore all the modalities to find what resonates with you. It can be one or like myself multiple modalities that works for your needs.

Thank you to all who have been a part of my journey and supported or encouraged me to be more than I am. Mom and Dad, my daughter, sister, niece and nephews. Numerous friends, teachers and encouragers. Bless you all.

All poems are my original work.

ABOUT THE AUTHOR: TAMARA FAUST

 Tamara Faust started writing as a young girl as a way of expressing her thoughts and emotions. Her early work was poetry, finding comfort in the written word that she couldn't verbally express. Her first poems were published in the local church camp newsletter. She went on to be published in The International Library of Poetry. Her love of music and words eventually turned into songs.

Tamara is an Usui, Holy Fire and Karuna Holy Fire Reiki Master. She delights in feeling the energy of flower bouquets and crystals. Through the use of Reiki, crystals, and singing bowls, she uses these healing techniques to provide comfort to others. Her passion is bringing awareness of the many modalities of healing and teaching everywhere she goes. She enjoys small adventures with her dog, Smoke, and warm cuddles with her cat, Tobin. Her daughter, son-in-law and three grandsons live a day's drive away, and she is always grateful to spend time with them. Additionally, Tamara can be found buried in a book, behind the camera or seeking new insights in her travels. While content in the present, she is excited to see what awaits around the next corner.

FOUR

Dancing with Dis-Abilities

By Kris Hansen

Day after day blurred into the next, until I found myself rushing to get to work at the hospital, fast walking down the long hospital hallway to the recovery room where I worked three twelve-hour shifts a week. I can remember the sound of my nursing scrubs brushing up against each other at my thighs and the feel of my rushed breath as I scurried through the automatic doors. I was not feeling any emotion. Nothing. Like numb, but at the time I wasn't aware of that. I just needed to get to work on time.

Once my shift began, I started talking with one of my coworkers. She was having some troubles with a family member, and I listened to her discuss her problems as if I would be solving EVERYTHING. Like I had all the answers. I started talking rapidly, and my body felt hot, and my face got sweaty. I was talking so loudly and so quickly that I found myself yelling. My ears felt hot, and the sounds around me became muffled. My jaw was open. I was yelling, right there in front of everyone, about this coworker's issue, as if it was my own issue. I was outraged. Repulsed by this horrible thing happening, and I was going to make it right. I was going to fix it right there and give everyone a piece of my mind! I felt like I was fighting for my own life, like survival. A terrible, horrible, red-hot feeling in my chest, like something ripping through me, took over. Anger. Pain. Utter outrage. I was justifiably out of control, yelling uncontrollably, and I didn't even know what I was yelling.

Then, out of nowhere and to my own surprise, I got quiet and acutely aware that I was acting out of my mind. Completely crazy. I saw it on people's faces around me - their eyes appeared wider than they should, filled with surprise and alarm. Facial expressions of shock registered in my brain. People were actively moving me away from the front of the recovery room, escorting me to a quiet room.

"Kris, I think you have cracked," said my nurse friend. "You just blew your stack about someone else's problems."

I certainly had, and what was that outrageous being that overtook me? Was *that* my mama bear coming out? I realized that I needed help, that I needed to calm down, and that I'd never been so embarrassed in all my life. How was I ever going to show my face again in that place? What must my nurse friends think of me now? I didn't even apologize. I didn't finish my shift. I couldn't get out of that recovery room quickly enough.

After that day, everything was different. It was as if, from that moment on, I had woken up to discover just how shut down and detached I was. That was when the mama bear woke me up. That embarrassing moment of truth brought my world crashing down and left me standing in the rubble of a life I had survived for the past eighteen months. I was finally awake. I was now aware of, (and filled with extreme shame about), how bottling up emotions and cutting myself off from my own humanity produced this pressure.

It was the end of November, and my husband and I were approaching eight months of hard work getting our eight-month-old off tube feeding. Lucien had been born in an emergency c-section and came home after six weeks spent in the NICU (neonatal intensive care unit). He was in the NICU because he had complications from lack of oxygen to his brain at birth. He also had a series of neurological issues and a problem called "persistent fetal circulation" that caused some heart damage. Big words like Periventricular Leukomylasia and Hypoxic Ischemic Encephalopathy were tossed around by NICU doctors. The day we came home from the hospital with Lucien, my dad called me to tell me he was going to have a brain tumor removed the next day. He and my stepmom had kept it from me because of all the stress I was under with Lucien, my newborn first child was in the NICU. Even during my daily calls to my stepmom while Lucien was hospitalized, she never mentioned my dad being sick. I think she was being merciful.

Lucien was in physical therapy and feeding therapy while being tube fed instead of breast fed (I pumped), and eight-months in, we were weaning him off many medications. It was exhausting as new parents, with all the monitors, equipment, appointments, and medications... but I was a nurse! I could handle it! When in a state of crisis, other people can fall apart, but I was a nurse. I could handle this! No time for crying. We had a goal. We were going to get Lucien off tube feeding and start to work on his crawling. We had a plan. I was working full time every other day while my husband, Rob, worked opposite of me so we could take care of Lucien. Lucien was a happy baby with lots of problems, but at least he was alive and thriving, and we were making progress. In fact, we never found out why Lucien ended up so sick at full term, we just knew we needed to get him to full oral feedings. That was the goal, and it was almost as if meeting this goal would make everything right. We could then put this whole beginning-birth experience behind us.

The week of Thanksgiving, eighteen months into Lucien's life, we closed on our first home and moved in. I stayed focused on the millions of things we had to do, the overwhelming process of packing up our two-bedroom apartment and moving forty-five minutes away to our newly built three-bedroom home. My ten-year-old dog, Malachite, had become progressively sick in the last few months, and despite all medical care, my rat terrier dog was dying. I was too busy to register how heartbroken I was to lose this relationship with my beloved Mal Mal, to realize that he wasn't going to join us in our new home. This was my way to shield myself from yet another overwhelming grief. I was too busy to register much of anything. The new house, moving, losing my dog, and there was more to come…and I was just being busy in my head instead of allowing any of it to sink in, register, move me, and absorb. I was fine on the outside.

I kept saying that I was fine, even when my mom was distraught that she wasn't going to be there for me in this move. My mother and stepdad had been there for us so much in these last eighteen months. My mom would help clean the house, get groceries, and watch Lucien. Joe, my stepdad, had just been diagnosed with liver cancer that November. While we were getting ready to move, he was receiving chemo. It was okay because I was fine. That same week we had to take Malachite to the veterinarian. He was miserable and in so much pain. I couldn't even take him to relieve himself on the grass. He could only get to the patio. I was afraid he would bite Lucien because he was in so much pain and had become so mean. He was not the same dog I knew for so many years. I knew it was time to say goodbye to my first "baby."

My beloved Malachite, the dog who stood by me while I went through everything: a bad first marriage to a drug addict, divorce, singlehood adventures, new love, a second chance at marriage, and the birth of my first born. In his last few days, Malachite was not the same doggie baby I had loved all those years. My fur baby was broken, and no matter what we gave him for pain, his condition worsened. When the vet offered a surgery that would cost $3,000 and came with no guarantees of success, we had to face the fact that we didn't have that kind of money. In the end, I chose to give him his final release from his body. My heart broke while taking him into that room and holding his paw while the vet stopped his suffering. All I could think about while holding his little lifeless body was his blanket. If they would just take his blanket with him into the back area...I didn't want him to be uncomfortable on a cold hard surface. When he left, I cried. I cried so hard. But because my husband was in the waiting room with Lucien, and we needed to get on with our busy week, I dried my tears. I said my goodbyes and shoved all that pain down deep inside of me, and I walked out of that room, leaving my poor doggie there. I sucked it up. I pushed it down. I packed it in tightly. I was needed for my son, this move, our little family.

That week we moved into our new home, and I squeezed in a follow-up visit with Lucien's pediatrician. At that point, my husband and I were so happy that Lucien was finally off tube feeding, but there were still many specialists to see because Lucien was a baby who was in the NICU. We took him to appointments after appointments, but there I was holding Lucien on the raised exam table talking to the pediatrician who looked down at my son's tightly scissored little legs.

"Oh, that's Cerebral Palsy," she said in the most matter-of-fact voice.

I reacted immediately, like: *How did I not know that?* I'm a nurse. Of course that's cerebral palsy. Why wouldn't I know that? My son has cerebral palsy. MY SON has cerebral palsy. Lucien has cerebral palsy (CP). What does that mean? I don't know what the pediatrician said after that. I was lost in my own thoughts. I couldn't comprehend anything. How could this be happening?

That same week my mother became a widow. Joe died after two days in hospice. No Thanksgiving meal that year. I drove from work to see him in hospice for the last time on Thanksgiving night. My mother had not eaten that day. I begged the nurses for something they could give her because no restaurant was open on Thanksgiving Day. Everyone was at home with their families celebrating while my mom was saying goodbye to the man who loved her for the last thirty years. By this time, I couldn't cry. I was seeing things happening, but I wasn't registering any of it as *sad*. I wasn't feeling anything. I was walled off from emotion. I didn't even know what was happening. I was Pink Floyd, "Comfortably Numb," robotically doing the next right thing, detached from world around me and the pain anyone was feeling. I needed to be there for my patients, my husband, my child, my mom, like there *physically* to help in any way I could, but I was GONE emotionally. I was bobbing away in my life vest on a sea of loss after loss after loss.

I was Daddy's good little girl. I loved my dad. The memories I have of him coming home after work are precious. As a little girl, it was like a celebration. "Daddy's home! Daddy's home!" I would run to the door, and he would lift my little body as light as a feather up into his big burly arms. I would sink my little fingers into his thick rug of a beard and scratch it like I was scratching a big bear's furry hide. He would growl low and then explode with laughter. Both of us giggling in the joy of reunion. As I grew up, he taught me how to drive defensively. He taught me how to stay safe as a young lady in "this big bad world." He taught me many useful home improvement things. It's like every time we were together, he would be showing me what he was doing and the rationale behind why he was doing it that way. He was always teaching me.

My father never kept a grudge about anything. Even when I was a young adult on my own and didn't call him for an entire year because I was "too busy." I picked up the phone because I had just done a self-development program that had me thinking about how much I loved my dad and how much of a selfish, emotionally stingy person I was…I called him up…wishing that he wouldn't pick up the phone. When he did, I launched into my childhood memory of him and how much I wanted to have a relationship with him. After blurting out that childhood memory on the phone with him and gushing out, "Dad, I love you, I'm sorry I haven't called. I want to have a close relationship with you again!" I waited for his response like I was waiting for the other shoe to drop. After a few moments of agonizing silence, he just said, "Yeah, Kris, sure!" Like nothing had ever happened. As if I had never waited a year to call him. From that point forward, every call was like my "Daddy's coming home" celebration.

Six weeks after the loss of my fur baby, my son's CP diagnosis and my stepdad dying, my father died in hospice from a second brain tumor. I got the call that he was going to have another surgery for his returning brain tumor, so I flew to Michigan to say goodbye to him and be there for his death and funeral. I held his hand. I told him it was okay to go, that I would take care of his bride as if she were my own mom. I made sure he got everything he needed at the hospital. I helped my stepmom prepare, helped her arrange the funeral and got all his pictures together. The day of my dad's funeral, my husband picked a fight with me over the phone. I don't remember what it was about. I just remember feeling very alone. Rob was the only person who had my back was being petty and not supporting me. I know in the back of my mind that my husband was dealing with Lucien, with work, and with being home alone with no back up while I was away for a week. Still, I had no compassion for him at all. I had begun building my brick wall around me, and I couldn't deal with my husband anymore. So, I walled off Rob as if he were the enemy. I said my father's eulogy. I visited with my family. I walked through my life asleep. Not feeling despair, depression, or sadness. Totally walled off.

It was not until nearly half a year later when that mama bear ripped through my chest and emerged in the recovery room and woke me up, that I found out how lost I was. On that day, my expectations—of motherhood, marriage, sacrifice, loss, and even life itself—were altered.

I once read a poem about an expectant mom traveling to Italy. Having a baby is like planning a glorious trip to Italy. Learning the language and reading all the books about the Sistine Chapel, Michelangelo, the Roman Empire, and the Colosseum. So much excitement and joy for what's to come, and the day I got on the plane to have my little buddle of joy, I landed in Holland. Not Italy. I was supposed to be in Italy with the Amalfi Coast. I was supposed to be eating Gelato and visiting the Cathedral of Santa Maria del Fiore in Florence.

"Welcome to Holland' - By Emily Perl Kingsley

When you're going to have a baby, it's like you're planning a vacation to Italy. You're all excited. You get a whole bunch of guidebooks, you learn a few phrases so you can get around, and then it comes time to pack your bags and head for the airport.

Only when you land, the stewardess says, "WELCOME TO HOLLAND."

You look at one another in disbelief and shock, saying, "HOLLAND? WHAT ARE YOU TALKING ABOUT? I SIGNED UP FOR ITALY."

That's what it feels like to have a special needs child. I wasn't in Italy.

I was in the Holland from the poem, lost in a new language,

surrounded by unfamiliar people and places, and completely unprepared. Everyone who was in Italy reported back their excitement about their expected children and how they were having all those experiences I wanted to have. They had their experiences with those perfect little babies. I was stuck in Holland desperately wanting the perfect Italian vacation, holding onto pictures in my mind of what it was supposed to be, and hoping at some point, I could get to Italy. Giving up layer upon layer, year after year, missed milestone after milestone, of what childhood development should be like—of what I wanted but couldn't have.

Lucien had cerebral palsy. Lucien had brain damage. Lucien wasn't going to have a "normal life." He wasn't going to drive, go to a regular high school, date, fall in love, get married, have kids of his own. He wasn't going to go to college, gett a job, make money, have a business, buy a house, drive a car, be a productive member of society. Lucien was going to have therapies and be cared for around the clock. He would never be an "adult" no matter how many years he was alive on this earth. Lucien would be a custodial care person, in *my* care, all his life. Unless I institutionalized him, he was never leaving home. I didn't know the totality of what I'm writing about here because at this point in my story, Lucien was eighteen months old, and I still had hope. I had hope back then that the right drug, therapy, or process was going to turn Lucien around. Now, years later into the experience of motherhood, I see that year after year, raising Lucien was like waiting for Lucien to become "normal." As I write this, Lucien is nineteen years old.

The grief was unbearable.

The thought of caring for someone for the rest of my life, no matter what happened, was inconceivable. It's not natural. It's not fair. And then what happens after I'm gone? Who is going to care for him then? I knew what happened to the people who had no one to care for them. They end up in state- and locally operated nursing homes. With patient-to-nurse ratios so high, no one gets any personal attention, ever. I couldn't face the facts because the facts were just so overwhelming, so painful, so real, with no real options for escape. So, back then, I pretended it was all going to be okay so I didn't have to face these cold hard facts.

We were coming home from my mom's house one Sunday afternoon, and Lucien started to seize in my husband's arms. Lucien was eighteen months old at this point. He didn't feel warm, and we didn't know what was going on. My husband quickly got through the door, put him on the floor of our foyer, and Lucien stopped breathing, turning blue. Rob looked up at me with panic in his tear-soaked eyes and said, "I can't feel a pulse." I looked down at Rob and pulled my mama bear out from my core and screamed, "Start CPR NOW!" and he jumped right into it. I ran to the phone, but it wasn't on the dock. I ran to the other dock, but the phone wasn't there either. I frantically looked around the house for the phone to call 911. WHERE WAS THE PHONE?! I scrambled to the floor and found it, but it was dead, because it wasn't on the charging dock. So, I threw it with all my might across the room. It hit the wall with force and broke into pieces. I found my cell, in my purse, with one bar left and dialed 911, my hands shaking uncontrollably. My mind raced unlike anything I had ever experienced in any code blue situation at work. COME ON COME ON COME ON, screamed in my head. I waited FOREVER for the call to pick up. In the back of my head, I was hearing an instructor's voice saying, "Pediatric cardiac events never go well in the field." The same voice screamed out my address as soon as the operator answered. I was shrieking. My heart pounded so hard; I could not think. I was watching my baby die on the floor of my own home.

I never want to hear myself screaming like that ever again. I can't even recognize that voice in my memory as my own voice. By the time the ambulance arrived, we had revived Lucien, but he was unconscious. The paramedic scooped him up off the foyer floor and whisked him to the nearest emergency room. At the hospital, we were given some medication to give him if he were to have another seizure, sent home, and told that it was probably febrile seizures and to make sure we kept Tylenol around. These events lead us to a cardiologist, a gastroenterologist, a neurologist, a pediatrician, a physical therapist, an occupational therapist, a vision therapist, and a speech therapist. I was researching everything I could about cerebral palsy and how to help us navigate the world of special needs. I thought that knowledge would save me and that learning everything I could, finding every resource out there, would make the difference. So I was exhausting myself in my quest to leave no stone unturned. I had to keep going. I ate Ramen noodles, candy bars, pasta noodles, and Pop Tarts and soda, stuffing myself with whatever I could get to move through my day. I don't think I was ever present with Lucien or Rob during those days.

Lucien seized again, in his sleep, and after another ambulance ride, I watched my baby seize for two hours and thirty-eight minutes before they could stop it with the right combination of IV medications. He was life flighted to the children's hospital when the seizures stopped. We were in the pediatric intensive care unit (PICU) for a few days. There he was strapped down, with wires coming from everywhere, stuck on a ventilator, and *not* sedated. My husband and I helplessly watched him suffer from his bedside, singing every song we knew until we were hoarse. When your child is that sick, you don't leave their side. You don't get a break. I labored under some delusions that I knew anything because I was a nurse. Nothing technical makes sense when you are the parent, no matter what your profession. Seizure medications and more specialists added to the growing list.

I knew I needed to bring Lucien a sibling. Lucien needed a protector if I wasn't going to be there at some point in Lucien's life. I chose bringing James into our family three years after

Lucien was born. I just went off my birth control without consulting Rob. That's how disconnected I was from marriage as a partnership. Rob was happy I was pregnant. I never told him that it was planned. Laying in the bed at the hospital after my first c-section to deliver Lucien, I had a vison of a baby boy about two years old toddling through the grass in the back yard, and I knew there was another person I was supposed to mother. (Not at all excusing my lack of partnership by saying I had this vision.) I can't justify my lack of responsibility to Rob.

I laugh now when I wrestled with the idea that I had the power to tell God to give me that long overdue trip to Italy with James. When James was born, I landed in Holland, with another foreign list of diagnoses and specialists to see. Autism, anxiety, sensory issues, and ADHD are the diagnoses we deal with now. It is easier the second time around being in Holland as a foreigner. I knew more about what to expect. I now know that diagnoses are opportunities for more doors to open to specialty services. I embrace the differences without feeling too isolated from society. I remind myself that I am just like any other parent. I want my children to have a great life and to be happy, content, and to learn how to live life fully. I ask questions. I learn to advocate for my children without being rude, mean, or accusatory. I know I don't have all the answers, so I spend most of my time connecting with others and building partnerships, creating teams, to support our boys. Holland might be where special needs parents end up, and Italy might be where parents with neurotypical children reside. The two countries don't need to be that far apart.

Today, I still search for best practices, the best ways to provide for Lucien and James. I have become an advocate for them, and I have since dedicated my life to health and wellbeing—physically, mentally, emotionally, and spiritually. I have amassed a small army of resources, tools, and techniques for communicating with educators and health providers. I have connected with other special needs parents to support them and to give back for all that was given to me, and to share the things that we had won through suffering.

In the last five years, I found powerful phytonutrients (from a company called Juice Plus+) that have increased Lucien's expressive and receptive language skills. Lucien even said the words, "I love you" for the first time to me after six weeks of taking these phytonutrients. It has also helped James with schoolwork and attention. I now find happiness and satisfaction sharing with other parents the powerful tools I have discovered on my journey. My joy is in assisting other special needs parents navigate Holland. I do that through social media posts, sharing resources, and pointing to important solutions that have helped our tribe.

The potent balm of compassion and deep acceptance created in this crucible of loss and suffering, helped soothe my sorrow since those beginning dark years. From the day that mama bear woke me up out of my thousand-mile-stare, I was becoming something. Every layer of grief peeled back a layer of inauthenticity with it, and I became a hollowed vessel. That vessel has become a receptacle of love and compassion that fills up from my spiritual development. I am always in a state of healing, surrendering, healing, and rebirth. The paradox breaks my heart of knowing I will either leave this earth with Lucien still here, agonizing over who is going to love and protect him when Mommy isn't here (James, of course, will provide great support and love for Lucien), OR I will witness the death of my child in my lifetime. I don't get to pick which one will happen, but one of them *will* happen. And I surrender to this suffering every day. I also plan and prepare for both scenarios. I know that there is no true way to fully prepare for your child's death.

My healing started as a process of letting go. Letting go of preconceived ideas, for example...is there really an Italy out there? Is there really a "normal" child out there? Don't all parents have to parent their children differently than others? I had to let go of the notion that discovering knowledge would save me or my children from further challenges, that knowledge would save the day. My marriage crumbled under the weight of special needs parenting. When everything I held dear to me was stripped from me, I found new meaning, new perspectives. For example, I thought you had to be married to have one family. You don't. I thought you had to have "normal" kids and go on vacations to Italy to be happy. You don't. I thought you had to be married to honor your marriage vows. You don't.

I could see that holding onto the prediction of what will happen in life is arrogant and rather vain. Having children is like shooting an arrow out and not knowing where it will land. I have learned that many special needs parents uncover a simple truth early on the path of parenthood—that our children are not really ours, and their fate is not resting on us. We are stewards of our children. A good portion of our children's path has nothing to do with us. It's all an illusion to think that their futures can be orchestrated by us. It's their lives, not ours. God has planned the boys' paths, and I am here to support them and be their earthly mother.

When James was born, my husband and I no longer shared a marital connection. Sure, we connected when we focused on caring for Lucien and our new baby boy, but the stress and strain of everything had taken its toll on both of us and our relationship. At one point, I found myself alone, caring for what I considered three boys (not two boys and a husband), working, and maintaining the inside and outside of our house. I was drowning. I craved a way out. Now, this didn't mean that my husband was unhelpful or uncaring. In fact, I knew that he loved me deeply, but we were choosing different reactions to handle the stresses we faced. We were two *very* different people. The walls I built up to survive were not going to let anyone in. I alienated Rob, and he was drowning, too. He ended up in a full-blown emotional tailspin by the time James was six months old, having to be placed in a psychiatric hospital for a week to stabilize on medications and get help for his obsessive-compulsive disorder. This was new, as I didn't know he had a psychiatric past. Rob was always a bit anxious and "a loner" who had some social anxiety, but Rob couldn't come out of our bedroom one day because a nurse for Lucien brought raw chicken into the house. Rob couldn't be around raw chicken. He feared everything was contaminated. He would not touch anything. Rob lost eight pounds in a week from not eating and barely drinking water. I had to take him to the hospital to admit him, and I was resentful towards Rob instead of compassionate because I had to take care of him and two boys while working fulltime. There was no self-care.

Rob and I may not have agreed on our own relationship, but we agreed on what we would do for our children. I had found some places throughout the country that were specifically engineered to care for children with seizure disorders, cerebral palsy, intellectual disabilities, and global delays. I wanted to find a place that would give Lucien and James better educational opportunities, and for Lucien, better complex medical care. There was a cerebral palsy clinic by the Delaware/Pennsylvania border that looked promising, so in 2008, I moved out of my home and took high-paying traveling nurse contracts in another city to raise the money to move our family. I was separated both physically and maritally from Rob, and I worked almost every day of the week as a nurse for more than a year. When I wasn't at work, I threw myself into transformational work with a company called Landmark Worldwide. I read, slept, worked, and participated in the self-development programs (or whatever you want to call them), and then traveled back and forth between two cities to visit my children when I could, which wasn't often. I was racked with enormous mommy guilt for not being there. My body ached to see them. I questioned myself every day.

In the communication program, the concepts of a tribe, co-parenting, and one family was born. Rob and I could remain a

family, even without marriage. It was messy. But we had two
special needs children, and our differences were going to take
a back seat to more important people in our life: Lucien and
James. In the mess of our crumbling marriage and the birth of
one family, we started to create a game called "everybody wins."
Sounds weird to be playing games with each other during the
breakup of our marriage. Right. It was a way we could meet
each other on a different field. The field of cooperative parallel
play. We decided to play to our strengths and what defined us as
parents. I didn't think putting my kids to bed every night defined
me a mom, while Rob reported that he would be broken if he
didn't live with his kids. So, the kids lived with Rob as I worked
as a nurse and provided for them. I could make more money as
a nurse that brought in better financial choices for us as a family.
Rob stayed home to be the primary caregiver to the boys. We
lived in two separate apartments in the same complex.

Once my family - or co-parented family - or unconventional
family - whatever you want to call it - had settled into life in our
new city, I started to take down my wall in the weirdest of all
places - an online game.

Through friendship that started as buddies in an online game,
I knew John as a geek in this game I played to escape reality.
Running around with my online buddy as avatars, I learned to
be who I truly wanted to be, just in a digital form. This gave me
freedom to try on new ways of being. The creative world helped
me form new connections, travel, and explore within a digital
environment. It broke me out of my protective shell from behind
my wall. The area where Rob and I and the kids eventually
moved was in the same town as my computer geek friend, John.
It all seemed so serendipitous. A year later, John and I fell in love
during a business training program. I became insanely jealous of
him and accused him of flirting with my friend! It was time to
open myself back up to love and share how I felt about him. That
took massive amounts of courage. Through that program, the

participants all called John "Captain Jack." Maybe it was from his years of sailing.

One very hot June day in 2012, we were married on the Spirit of Philadelphia in a wild pirate wedding attended by our friends, all dressed as pirates. Pirates jousted each other with fake swords, the pirate troupe from a local renaissance festival "conscripted" everyone onto the boat into their pirate way of life. A lot of pirate jokes and "arrhhhgggss" were heard that day. We had that pirate wedding, celebrating love and commitment in community. For our marriage, we have three agreements and one context for our marriage: (1) Always be complete (2) Listen to each other as great (3) Play the game "I want what you want" (so we are always walking the same path) and the context is playing a game greater than ourselves. John is my compass, and I challenge him to pull up his anchor and set sail out of the safe harbor to whatever adventures await us on the open seas.

Several people have shared their beliefs and stories with me through the years. I believe they want to help me because being a special needs parent is a daunting task, and I'm sure they want to support me in any way they can. I have kept all the stories, but I feel one of them is closest to my truth about Lucien and James. I can't remember who told me this one, but it is by far my favorite.

There was a war in heaven, between good and evil, before we all came to the Earth. Lucien was a major general in this war. When Lucifer fell, he cursed all the generals, that they would all fall to evil as men on the Earth if they came down here and took a human form. James was a gallant protector of the generals. God protected Lucien and sent him here without his agency—to be served, loved, protected, and cared for all his days. James was given to Lucien as his protector. That is why I had that vision and knew there was another child to be born of our family. Lucien is unable to choose evil. Because he doesn't have his agency, he has no need to be saved because he is forever innocent. Lucien has the golden ticket to heaven, back to his Heavenly Father, and he is protected by his brother, James. Lucien is here to teach us all the true meaning of service and joy.

Our tribe, our one family, has changed since my marriage to John. James needed more individualized help in 2018. More help than Rob could provide while still supporting Lucien's needs. James moved in with me and John, creating shared custody with Rob (we all moved into a townhouse community together with Rob and the kids in one home and John and I in another). James would spend half the time with us and the rest with his father and brother. When the pandemic shut down schools, Lucien stayed with Rob and James stayed with us fulltime. This was to ensure Lucien's safety since he was considered a high risk for poor outcomes should he contract covid.

I was working at a desk as a nurse case manager for a big health system. That system gave each desk nurse an option to go on unpaid leave, lose their jobs, or go back to the bedside to assist with the first wave of covid patients. I went to the ICU, having never touched a patient in ten years. Scared to death, unprepared for the horrors, and ten years older with no up to date bedside skills, I bought some scrubs and comfy shoes. I went back to the bedside. That part of the story is for another time, except to say, all but four patients died in those six weeks of bedside service. It was like a war zone. Not enough caregivers, not enough supplies, not enough medication. It was the beginning of the end of my nursing career. I have PTSD from that experience. I still see a therapist three years later. And I did retire from my 30-year nursing career in 2022 to become an affiliate marketer fulltime.

The day before I was to start my shifts at the temporary ICU job that April, Rob called me asking me to come see him because he didn't feel too good. Prior to this, I had been shopping for Lucien and Rob, making sure they didn't have to leave the town house for anything. Just to keep them safe. I visited Lucien at the sliding glass doors in the back of their townhouse as our barrier every couple of days. This day, I went to the front door to look at Rob from a distance. He appeared yellow, sickly, with a large mass on his left shoulder. My stomach knotted up. Wide eyed I said, "Rob, pack your bag you are in liver failure, you need to go to the hospital right now." I raced back to my townhouse and told John to come sit with Lucien that I needed to take Rob to the ER. I thought he had some kind of blood cancer judging from the large mass and his jaundiced skin color.

It was many days, many conversations with the medical team, and tests when we found out Rob had stage IV non-Hodgkin's lymphoma with a 70% chance of recovery. I moved in with Rob to care for Lucien and then I ended up caring for Rob as his health declined. And the chemo didn't work. And neither did the three other regimes the doctors tried. With each new plan of attack, the chance of a cure dwindled. And then he got sicker, losing his ability to walk, eat, or be comfortable even on high doses of narcotics. He managed the whole month of August to read Lucien's favorite books to him recorded on YouTube just to be sure Lucien could remember his dad, should Rob not make it. Rob had to be hospitalized by the end of September 2020. Not long into the hospitalization, I got the call in the middle of the night that he had a complication and was hanging on by a thread in the ICU.

The doctors could do no more for him. He was on full life support to keep his heart pumping. He was still conscious, so I took photos of the boys to share with Rob. I took special cards for Rob to sign for our son James to cherish throughout special milestones in James' life because Rob wouldn't be there in person for those. Rob and I called everyone important to him so he could say goodbye. We called Rob's father in New York. We called Rob's pastor, who he was so close to him during Rob's cancer battle. We took pictures. John brought James up to see his father one last time. We Facetimed Lucien so Rob could see and talk with Lucien. I watched an episode of The Office together at Rob's request, his favorite TV show. I got Rob a soda with that special hospital ice that makes drinks so cold and perfect. Rob said after he drank it, that it was the best drink he'd ever had. We held hands as Rob started to drift off, letting the sedative drugs take effect. Rob woke up at one time and said, "Boo!" He was thinking he was a ghost, and he was going to scare me. I laughed. We smiled at each other. He said, "I love you." And I said, "I love you too". Then he slipped into another state, not here but not unconscious. He was talking long sentences to other people, no one that I could see in the room with us. His voice became weaker and muffled then mumbling imperceptible to me. John joined me in the room, after taking James back home, as Rob slipped away into full unconsciousness. John held my hand as I held Rob's hand as Rob passed away. I kissed him on his forehead to say goodbye to the father of my children, the funniest man I ever knew, one of our tribesmen, and the person I knew I still loved even though we couldn't stand each other being married. I had honored my wedding vow to Rob, I loved him till death do us part. It took losing Rob to realize that I loved him.

It has been a challenge coming out of covid lockdown, helping my children grieve, and navigating life with two special needs young men without Rob. I have had to seek help for PTSD using medications and counseling. Everyone in our tribe has been affected. John and I have had to work double time to stay on the same page instead of working against each other. My mom lives with us and helps us with Lucien and the house. James has been in grief counseling, navigating his anger and sadness. Lucien has had some awful moments begging for his Daddy and wailing out of sadness.

You may have watched Lucien and I on social media, singing songs or reading books. I share his joy with the world because Lucien does not separate himself from us. He doesn't recognize himself as separate. He is one with us. He is one with the eternals. When you get to be with Lucien, you get to experience being one with all. It's magical. It's therapeutic. I see Lucien as he should be. As he is. And as he is not. When I see his challenges now, they don't bring up feelings of loss or grief. I don't long for Italy anymore.

I love Holland. It has stone bridges with beautiful windmills. Tulips that stretch farther than the eye can see. And Rembrandts. He is having an awesome ordinary life. He knows the joys of life. James is a young man with a passion for flying airplanes (before even getting his driver's license). He loves video games and YouTube. James receives straight A's in his classes. Lucien lives in the present. He doesn't worry about the future. He expresses joy without reservation. People come up to me at the local pool to thank me for bringing Lucien, because his joy is infectious in every good way. Lucien lives a great life with a disability. He is a brother, a son, a grandson, a young man, a son of a Heavenly Father, a lover of Star Wars and music of all kinds (Johnny Cash and the Beatles are at the top of a long list). When I sing with Lucien, laughing and swaying in the air, dancing in the sheer joy of life, I often wonder who is the disabled one.

ABOUT THE AUTHOR: KRIS HANSEN

Kris Hansen lives in West Chester, Pennsylvania, with her eternal husband, John, her mother, Karen, and her two sons, Lucien and James. She is a retired nurse and a full-time online affiliate marketer and Founder Candidate with the Great Discovery. Kris participates in her local church currently preparing and teaching lessons for her fellow Relief Society Sisters. She loves to pamper her friends, play ball with her dog, Scout, and plan trips with her family. She cares for her elderly mom who still watches and plays with Lucien every evening. She owns an aloof cat named Bex who used to be Kris' late (former) husband, Rob's cat. She assists Lucien in his awesome and ordinary life and prepares James to launch into his late teens and early adulthood life with the strong partnership of Team Rainbow (that's John and Kris' name for their marriage). Kris' lifelong passion for self-development has led to forming a strong relationship with a new program of self-improvement.

To find out more about the Great Discovery, a course that teaches a proven way of thinking to produce results and be effective/successful in life (and any endeavor you choose to take on):

www.thegreatdiscovery.com/kris123
You can reach Kris by emailing: kristhebliss@gmail.com.

FIVE

A MOTHER'S JOURNEY: DANCING THROUGH LOSS

By Julie Powers

*M*y baby girl first died when she was three months old, and then she lived, and then she died again when she was eight and a half years old, and yet, she lives. How convoluted is this story? Am I a delusional mother who has lost her wits due to her daughter's death or is it possible that loss, death, grief and resulting life lessons can entangle themselves into a story of discovery, expansion, and joy? *Joy?* How is that possible?

How can I, as a mother, *not* lose myself in grief when my own flesh and blood made an unnatural leap in the normal life timeline and left the earth before her parents? Didn't she read the rule book? Parents are supposed to go first! That's just the way it's supposed to be. Emma Christine Powers broke the rules. She tore me open. She ripped me apart. She changed me. Then she put me back together by helping me see the bigger picture and urges me – without using any words – to look outside the boxes and limiting constructs and, most importantly, to look deep inside. To see past the black and white and to have an open mind and heart for all the grey areas. To allow myself to be the person I am *meant* to be, not what I believe others expect, and to connect the dots that I can't even see. She does most of this teaching after her death, and she doesn't give up when I'm resistant. How does she *do* that? Seriously? When Emma had successfully completed her mission here on earth, and she was finished being trapped in a physical body that was confined to a wheelchair while periodically fighting for breath, she transitioned to her eternal self without an earthly body on July 26, 2007. She's free from her restricted, broken body-shell and I'm *joyful* about her freedom.

How did we get to this point?

1999

After returning from my lunch break, a police officer was standing at my desk at the bank where I worked. After confirming my identity, he said that my child was in an ambulance on the way to the hospital, so I immediately started walking out of the office toward my car. The officer followed, telling me that he would drive me there. I said, "No need. I'll beat you there." He was saying more, but I had tuned him out, because I was already in the hospital in my mind. I suspected that my two-year-old son had fallen at daycare and broken something.

When I got to the Emergency Room, instead of finding my son there, I saw my three-month-old baby girl on a gurney in the trauma room, and she was a strange bluish grey color, her eyes were closed, and she was not moving. I was told that she had stopped breathing while at the babysitter's house and that her brain didn't have any oxygen for about ten to fifteen minutes. Fortunately, the babysitter had known infant CPR and had continued working on her until the paramedics arrived. Looking at her limp body in the hospital - I had never seen human skin that color before, and I was terrified: I felt as if my blood stopped pumping through my veins. After the team worked on her, they told me and my husband, Corey, that they had called for an Air

Evac helicopter to life-flight her to Cardinal Glennon Children's Hospital in St. Louis.

We wouldn't realize until later that this was the day our Emma Christine died: the original Emma. The normal-as-could-be baby girl we brought home from the maternity ward after being born three months earlier. The girl we visualized would one day run and play and ride bikes and sing into hairbrushes with her friends. The girl who would excel in school and take dance classes like her mom or play tennis or soccer like her dad. The girl who would argue with her big brother but look up to him because he would be her hero. The girl who would write stories and paint pictures and play a musical instrument and watch sunrises and sunsets with awe. The girl who would travel the world and go on to find her soulmate and live an abundant and fulfilling life. That girl was gone forever.

The days following Emma's oxygen deprivation and the resulting traumatic brain injury (TBI) were a blur of terror and confusion. Corey and I slept in five-minute blocks of time in the bedside chair in the Pediatric Intensive Care Unit (PICU). We watched helplessly as the doctors and nurses drew blood, injected medications, scanned her brain and worked around the clock to get Emma comfortable. Days turned into many weeks, and she was finally stable enough to take home, but she would never be the same. She came home with a permanent feeding tube, a suction machine, a sleep monitor, a machine for breathing treatments and multiple medications. She would require twenty-four-hour monitoring and care *for-the-rest-of-her-life*. We were told that may not be very long, as "most kids in this condition die from pneumonia." We were told to "expect this and nothing more" and to be prepared for many challenges, especially with our marriage.

Emma came home and she cried. A lot. A sad, soulful cry while her eyes remained closed, and her arms moved almost continuously in a circling motion in front of her neck and face. She needed chest percussions and deep suctioning regularly to keep her airway clear and to avoid pneumonia *because we knew really bad things could happen if she contracted pneumonia.* She required frequent physical therapy to keep the stiffness and spasms minimized. This was the new Emma. The old Emma was gone. Dead.

For the next eight years, we were a family. Corey, me, our two-year-old son, Ian, New Emma, and everyone else who became necessary in our updated world. We tried to create a *normal* home as much as we could, but we knew that it was far from normal. With a revolving door for nurses, physical therapists, occupational therapists, speech therapists, educational therapists, and a lot of extra family help, we learned to exist with other people in our home during our most private moments and to schedule our lives according to Emma's needs. Those were eight years of hope and prayers for a miracle. Eight years of exhaustion, lessons in patience and unconditional love, excessive sleep deprivation, strict schedules, hair-trigger reactions, interrupted conversations, hospital stays, surgeries, and procedures. Eight years of celebrations, family and school events, community support, new perspectives, and gratitude. Because Emma required so much care, we had a system in place whereby anyone caring for Emma kept track of everything: feedings, chest percussions, suctioning, medications, therapies, sleeping time, diaper changes, elimination details, holding and rocking time/back time/wheelchair time, and notes about each detail of her life. Many of Emma's home care team mentioned how helpful this system would be for the other families they worked with and that I should consider marketing it. I laughed and said, "When would I work on that, between three and four in the morning?"

Although Emma's developmental prognosis was very grim, we celebrated any advancement. With her dedicated care team through home and the Farmington, Missouri school district, Emma made some progress. There were times that she was clear about her desires by turning her head slightly to one side or by moving the direction of her eyes left or right. During the last year of Emma's life, Corey would hold her in the rocking chair and slowly and distinctly say "I-LOVE-YOU. One-Two-Three." while blinking his eyes deliberately three times. Blink. Blink. Blink. He would ask her to do the same. It was HUGE when she blinked her eyes three times while looking at Corey. It was unmistakable that she was telling her daddy that she loved him, and it happened several times.

Emma's occupational therapist, Sherri, had an exceptionally close connection with her. From the moment she first laid her hands on Emma's body, Sherri said she could literally feel a "whooshing" and that the room was *filled with angels surrounding Emma*, and she had never experienced anything like that before. While that vision of angels made my heart happy, my brain struggled to understand it. My firmly developed black-or-white belief system was entrenched. How could it be possible for her to feel that? What did it mean? I thought it was remarkable, and I was envious of this feeling Sherri experienced, but it was foreign to me. I felt as if Emma had already connected to the *other side:* She was *here and there* at the same time, but I didn't really know what that meant or how that was possible. It didn't fit into the boxes of my deep-rooted beliefs, so I wasn't sure what to do with that feeling.

Over the next eight years this devoted Christian friend felt as if she were being led to dive deeper into understanding this gift with Emma. Sherri tried to explain the subtle energy flow she could pinpoint inside Emma's body and how she was able to affect the flow even when her hands didn't make physical contact. Sherri said she felt that God was working through her, and she would ask me to *feel* it, too. I would get frustrated by my inability to *feel anything*. It seemed that I had constructed impenetrable walls around me so that I didn't get distracted by feeling. I could simply continue to do, do, do to keep things running smoothly for Emma and everyone around me. I believed I didn't have time to *feel*, so when it came to working directly with me, Sherri said it was too difficult to pierce through my crust. I didn't want to be an unfeeling robot, but I guess I had somehow settled into that role.

For most of my life, I'd been good at blocking things from my deepest self, and I don't even know how that began. Following Emma's brain injury, I constructed even thicker walls around my heart. Therefore, I was able to stay focused on the daily to-do lists without needing to pause for an emotional breakdown. I could check off a list of a *hundred* things each day with a real (or a fake-it-'til-you-make-it) smile on my face. This approach left no time for reflection about the fear, confusion, loss, trepidation, anxiety, or vulnerability that I could have, and should have, recognized, addressed, felt, accepted, and assimilated into my life. Instead, I ignored all of it and just kept moving forward. There was a tiny glimmer of hope buried deep inside, though. A pinpoint of light that seemed as if it wanted to illuminate these things so that I could *feel* and be connected. I wanted to have that. I just didn't have time for it.

My selfless and caring mom, who regularly helped us with Emma's care, is one of the most compassionate natural caregivers I know. There were days I would come home from work and my mom would be rocking Emma. Emma would be sleeping soundly in her arms, and my mom would be crying. "What's wrong?" I'd ask with urgency in my voice. "What happened?" I assumed something bad must have occurred to warrant the tears, but my mom would say, "Don't you ever just feel like crying, Julie? Doesn't this just break your heart? Why don't you cry?" I simply replied, "I can't cry, Mom. If I start crying, I may not be able to stop, and that can't happen. Lives literally depend on me, so I must keep going and just deal with it." Whether or not this was a good way to live life was irrelevant. This was the way I got everything done each day without blinking. At the end of the day, I could hold Emma in my arms and rock her for hours, and that physicality and motion would drain most of the tension from my body. However close I felt to her and loved her with all that

I was, I was always holding back a flood of emotions, because I was not willing to open those gates. I knew I wouldn't be able to function in my roles as care coordinator, mom, wife, employee, daughter, sister, friend, volunteer if I freed my emotions.

Over time, I built the walls thicker, and my reactions got quicker: life-saving reactions for Emma, but also my hair-trigger reactions to my husband and son and anyone in my line of sight. I started snapping and having very little patience for anything that wasn't *just right* the first time, because who had time to go back and do it again? Not me! My attitude, coupled with extreme sleep deprivation, shortened my fuse and I became a tightly wound bitch to the people I loved the most—and I was a machine.

I always was (and still am) a light sleeper. It's one of the traits that made me perfect for the job of "Emma's mom." Being able to awaken quickly when hearing the slightest change in Emma's breathing was not only helpful, but also lifesaving. Many nights I slept with a pillow over my head to muffle out some of the other sounds in the house, but I heard every breath from Emma, and when I sensed a change, I could jump out of bed and be at her side within two seconds, suctioning her airway and making sure she was okay. More than eight years of this had trained me very well to be responsible and alert around the clock, but it took a toll on my health.

Sleep deprivation and a bad diet of mostly junk food compressed my already short fuse, but I kept going-going-going and doing-doing-doing. We had a household to run, a daughter to keep alive, and a son to raise as normally as possible. Emma's medical helpers were in our house all the time, making it challenging to balance normal life. I built my walls thicker and thicker, because no one on Emma's healthcare team needed to see a chink in the armor. They needed to feel that everything was under control and running smoothly. This was long before social media became part of everyday life, but I can clearly see now that I was attempting to live inside a filter. It's just not sustainable.

There were times in Emma's last year on earth that we had to "bag her" which means we used a manual resuscitator to ventilate her and get oxygen flowing into her lungs. She would turn a grey/blue hue and have a frightened look in her eyes before becoming unresponsive until we could get her through the episode. One time is seared into my memory when Emma was struggling with her breathing. Her face drained all color and then became blank. Corey and Ian and I were all home with her. We laid Emma on the floor and used the bag to force oxygen into her lungs through the mask we placed over her mouth, while Ian, (who was ten years old at the time), held her hand and kept saying, "Just breathe, Emma. It's okay. Just breathe." Our family dog, Thor, stood nearby, watching quietly with his eyes glued to us while trying to get his head closer to Emma. It was a family affair.

The one time we attempted a family outing to the St. Louis Zoo, Emma stopped breathing enroute and as my mouth was on hers and I was breathing for her, we headed to the nearest hospital. She took her second helicopter ride that day, and the amazing professionals at Cardinal Glennon once again got her back to "stable" and she came home.

Later that year, my mom stayed with Emma overnight because I had hurt my back and I was afraid I wouldn't be able to pick Emma up if she needed me. The next morning, my mom told me about the amazing dream she had while Emma slept soundly all night:

In the dream, Emma woke up my mom saying, "Grandma, I want to get out of bed!" and Grandma was startled, and said, "Emma, are you talking?!"

"Yes, Grandma. I want to get out of bed!"

Grandma reached into Emma's bed and picked her up. Emma wrapped her arms and legs around her grandma and squeezed very tightly. Then Emma said she wanted to go outside and play.

In the dream I came home and asked, "Where is Emma? Why aren't you with her? She can't be alone!"

Grandma smiled and said, "Emma's in the backyard! She wanted to play!"

When we went to the door together in the dream, I saw Emma running through the backyard. She turned and waved and said, "Hi, Mommy!" Then she kept running and laughing.

A few days later, Emma started gurgling as she did many times while sleeping. Nurse Diane got up to suction her, and when she had the suction tube all ready, Emma coughed as she removed the Thermovent (the filter at the end of Emma's trach tube). She coughed up bright red blood, and it filled up the filter. Diane started suctioning her, but she couldn't get the blood out fast enough, and she had no idea where the bleed originated. She got the next-size-up catheter kit and called me on the intercom, telling me to come quickly, so I jumped into action.

"What's going on?" I was so confused. "Why is she bleeding?"

Diane, who was busy suctioning Emma, threw the phone to me when I ran into the bedroom. "Call 9-1-1! It's not stopping!"

Emma looked like a gunshot victim from a movie—there was so much blood soaking through her pink princess nightgown, filling the suction canister and staining the blanket. I was terrified that Emma was "bleeding out." The doctors had told us that because Emma's anatomy was unusual, the rigid trachea tube could, at some point, wear down the lining of the artery, and then it would be bad - fatal. *That* was what was flashing through my mind.

Emma's eyes were closed during all of this, so she didn't have the panic-stricken look on her face that accompanied her labored breathing episodes from the last two years. I kept 9-1-1 on the phone and used Diane's cell phone to call my parents and ask them to come NOW. I also called Corey at his hotel in New Jersey, where he was working that week. I gave him the quickest synopsis with a sense of urgency that this was unlike any of Emma's episodes we had experienced over the last few months. He told me he would be on the next plane to St. Louis.

The nurse moved Emma to my bed so that she and I could both work on her at the same time. Then she deflated Emma's "cuff" that helps seal off the rest of the space around her trach tube. Within fifteen seconds, the bleeding stopped, and the blood started to clot. I got the oxygen tank and the ambu-bag (a manual resuscitator or "self-inflating bag), and Diane started bagging her. The ambulance and fire department arrived, and that's when Emma woke up. Unfortunately, so did Ian, and he wandered down the hall and into the bedroom with all the emergency personnel. I told him to go with Grandma and Grandpa (who had arrived moments earlier). I'm not sure if he saw all the blood because he was half asleep.

I rode in the ambulance with Emma to the local hospital, and I asked for a transport to Cardinal Glennon immediately. The emergency room nurse kept bagging Emma to force oxygen into her lungs while I completed the necessary paperwork, and after a while, it got harder and harder to bag her. The nurse said she thought the trach tube was clogged up with dried blood and that we needed to replace it. I got nervous about that because I was afraid that if we got the old one out, Emma would start bleeding again, and we wouldn't be able to get the new one in. When we pulled out the old one, there was a long string of thick, gooey blood hanging on the end of it, and the tube itself was completely filled with dried blood. I had no idea how Emma was able to get any air into her lungs, but the new one was clear and we could tell right away that Emma was breathing better. I had to run hot water through the old tube and rub it between my fingers to break up the clots.

The helicopter team arrived at the hospital and Emma took her third life flight to St. Louis. This helicopter was very small, so I couldn't fly with her. My mom and I drove to St. Louis together and got there about fifteen minutes after Emma did. She was on a humidified trach collar and oxygen, but other than that, she was back to her normal self. A chest x-ray and scope didn't reveal where the bleeding originated, but the medical team found a tiny spot at the top of the trachea near the stoma (the hole in her throat) that could have been where a clump of cells called a granuloma may have broken off and popped a blood vessel. That could have caused all the bleeding, but now at the hospital, there was not a single bit of blood anywhere in Emma's throat! It was a miracle. Everything looked normal, and Emma was resting easily and breathing well, even when she was weaned down to room air. This made no sense after the events that got us to this point.

Since she was doing so well, I called the orthotist to see if she was in the hospital and if she happened to have Emma's new leg braces with her. We were supposed to see her later in the week, so now seemed to be a good time to check in. The orthotist was available and brought the braces for Emma to try on her new "legs." They were pink (of course) and had "girls with attitude" written all over them. The new braces just needed a few adjustments, and then we could pick them up on Friday when Emma was scheduled for multiple appointments.

Corey miraculously caught a flight from New Jersey to St. Louis and got to the hospital right before we were ready to pack Emma into the van for the strangely normal return trip home. Other than being very tired, she seemed to be feeling like herself. She was very relaxed, as if nothing unusual had happened that day. No physical signs of blood loss. Corey, Ian, Emma, and I were all in the house together that afternoon and evening. We took turns holding and rocking Emma while singing her songs, reading her books, and rubbing and kissing her arms and cheeks.

The next day Emma had a wonderful day with Nurse Sandy after spending a cuddly night with Nurse Diane. She got to go outside and swing for over an hour in her special swing with multiple straps to keep her tightly secured. My mom brought Emma a pink princess tiara and a pink necklace, bracelet, and ring to complete her attire. She wore it the whole afternoon, in celebration of making it through the day before. Corey showered her with kisses throughout the day and repeated the "I-LOVE-YOU, 1-2-3" blinking connection. I came home from work that evening and got to hold her in the rocking chair for over an hour while she "ate" through her feeding tube. That day, Emma was acting so normal, we really didn't know what to think of it.

When Nurse Nicole came to take care of Emma that evening, she got the whole story about the previous day. Everyone was incredulous and wondering how the extreme bleeding began and then just stopped. Emma had been having frequent episodes during which she couldn't breathe. Those episodes were frightening, but we executed the rescue plan flawlessly each time with the ambu-bag and the oxygen. Repeatedly, Emma came out of it and was okay, so we were getting rather numb to these events. We were in a routine of scary occurrences, but everything turning out okay in the end. We started thinking maybe Corey could have stayed in New Jersey to finish the work project after all, but with that unusual bleeding episode, it was different this time. Huge. It was a call to action for Corey to get home quickly.

Everyone was perplexed but thrilled that Emma was doing so well. Ian even had a friend over to spend the night, so Emma got to see her big brother and his friend running through the house and playing. She always seemed to enjoy her brother's antics, and when his friends were in the house, there was even more excitement before bedtime.

It was about two o'clock the next morning when Nurse Nicole called me on the intercom and told me to come quickly. I ran up the basement stairs and got to the room within seconds. Emma had begun bleeding again, and the blood was everywhere. Worse than Tuesday. I grabbed the phone and called 9-1-1 and ran down the hall to get Corey. There was a lot of blood coming out of her trach—and from her nose and mouth this time. I talked to the 9-1-1 operator and got the oxygen tank while Nurse Nicole kept suctioning. Corey grabbed Ian and his friend and took them to my parents' house right around the corner.

Emma's bleeding wouldn't stop. The ambulance arrived and the EMTs got Emma on the gurney and took her to the local emergency room. Corey rode in the ambulance with her this time, and I drove the van behind them. The bleeding stopped in the ambulance. Nurse Nicole stayed at the house to clean up the blood, and my mom stayed with the boys at her house. My dad picked up Emma's "Go Bag" with her extra trachs and other supplies and met us at the hospital where the staff was keeping Emma stabilized while waiting on Air Evac for her fourth helicopter ride to Cardinal Glennon. Corey told me to drive on to St. Louis and that he would stop at the house to get his license and some real clothes for us to wear in the hospital—we were in our pajamas.

I arrived at the hospital just moments after the helicopter landed and was in the emergency room when they wheeled Emma into the trauma room. The staff was ready for her, and they spent the next couple of hours keeping her stable. Corey arrived at the hospital about twenty minutes after me. We stood by Emma's side, holding her hand, and talking to her. Corey talked softly to her and helped her get her elevated heart rate to slow down. It appeared that Emma's stomach was bloated with air, so I tried to release it by using her feeding tube. There was very little air that released—instead, there was a lot of blood. Wherever that blood was coming from, it had gone down her esophagus and into her stomach. Her lips were so dry that I had to apply some of her "lipstick" (Emma loved to have Carmex on her lips to make them soft.).

She started to bleed again, and her heart rate and blood pressure weren't good. She received three units of blood and our dear nurse friend from our hometown was assigned to Emma's case. Other hospital staff members who had cared for Emma over the years were there to support us as well. When the clogged-with-dried-blood trach tube was replaced, the bleeding began again. Emma's primary physician called us for a heart-to-heart conversation. We had recently finalized Emma's Advance Directive with him, and now what we had put on paper was now reality staring us in the face. Until we received more information, we were still cautiously optimistic that this would be another freaky false alarm.

The surgical team suspected a pin-hole erosion in one of the arteries that went from clogged to bleeding and then clogged again. The only way to know was to search for it in the operating room. The scope itself would be very risky for her, and they said if they found the hole, they would have to cut into her chest and possibly her neck to fix the leak. Corey and I were both terrified and knew that we could not put our baby girl through that kind of surgery, and we didn't want her to leave us without us being by her side. (The surgeon had said that we would not be allowed in the operating room.) This was the moment of truth. We declined the procedure. I called my dad right away. "Dad, you and Mom and Ian need to get here now. We are not bringing Emma home."

The ER team put Emma on a ventilator and worked quickly to move her to a more comfortable room in the PICU. Our hospital friends stayed with us the whole time, including the ENT, Dr. Albers, who only left our side when we requested private time. When we arrived in the PICU, the doctor who originally treated Emma the day she had her traumatic brain injury eight and a half years earlier was just finishing his shift. He expressed his deep concern for our family and then Emma's second doctor in the PICU all those years ago started his shift. Both doctors had cared for Emma numerous times over the years when she was in the PICU, and they knew her well. We felt like we had come full circle.

I wanted to make Emma as comfortable as possible. I tried brushing her hair, but it was caked with too much dried blood. I gently washed her usually silky golden hair in the bed, removing as many tangles as possible. Corey and I spent time kissing her cheeks, rubbing her arms, and holding her hands, trying to lock in the feeling of her skin.

When my parents arrived at the hospital with Ian, Corey and I took our son into a separate room to talk to him while my mom and dad went to Emma. We told Ian that his baby sister was not going to come home with us because she was very sick and was going to die. We told him that he needed to tell her goodbye. "But there's a chance that she will get better!" he said, not wanting to believe us. We repeated that she would be going to heaven that day and would not be coming home with us, so Ian saw Emma and gave her kisses, and our family stood in Emma's room and talked to her, touched her, kissed her, and loved her for as long as possible. My parents took Ian to the waiting room because he wanted to draw Emma a "Get Well Soon" picture.

Corey and I stayed with Emma. Then the vent was removed and replaced with only oxygen, and there was no machine breathing for her anymore. She kept breathing slowly. She was trying, but it was so difficult. Each breath was a soft gasp. We held her hands and kissed her without ceasing. We told her about her golden hair and how she was a princess. We told her how much we loved her and how much her whole family loved her. We told her how happy we were to have had her in our lives for eight and a half years. We told her what a joy she was. We told her how she was the very best little sister for the very best big brother in the world. As time ticked away, Emma's breaths came slower and softer. With each gasp, our hearts skipped a beat. Emma opened her eyes for just a moment, and our words stumbled over one another as Corey and I talked over each other so that we began and finished each other's sentences, "Oh, baby girl, we're here. We're right with you. You've been so brave. You don't have to fight anymore. You can go to heaven with Jesus and the angels. You can be free. You can run and jump and swing and fly and dance! It's okay if you want to go. We're here."

We watched the monitors as the numbers decreased. The oxygen saturation was dropping, and yet, Emma kept trying. She was saying goodbye, too. She started to bleed again, but nothing like before. The blood was oozing up her trach tube, but it didn't come out this time. The nurse turned the monitor screen so we couldn't see the numbers anymore. We were holding our princess' hands, and her hands were contracting and squeezing ours intermittently. I was kissing her fingers while Corey was kissing her cheeks. Emma was there, and then, with that last breath, she was gone. Her body was in front of us, but her essence had flown away. The oxygen flow was turned off. The monitors were disconnected. Fifty-nine minutes after the vent was removed, Emma died. Dr. Albers and Nurse Doug never left the room, both with us the entire time, lending support when needed. After we said our final goodbyes, we reluctantly left her room and went out to tell my parents and Ian that she was gone. We all went back into Emma's room together. Ian wanted to see his baby sister one more time.

We couldn't have orchestrated Emma's last days any better. My mom had a beautiful dream experience during her last overnight stay with Emma. Corey was home and spent uninterrupted time with her when he normally would have been working out of state. My parents delayed a bucket list trip and were in town. Emma's most-loved home care nurses each had one full shift with her before her last trip to the hospital. Emma's special hospital staff members were all on duty that last day, and I had extra one-on-one time with my baby girl. Everyone was exactly where they were supposed to be.

Although our family knew we had captured borrowed time with our special girl, it was much too soon to say goodbye. Emma Christine Powers - the little girl who couldn't walk or talk inhabited a huge amount of space by touching an incredible number of lives with blessings, gratitude, patience and joy. Emma had left the earth that day, but not our hearts. The loss that gripped my heart was as if a piece of me had been ripped out of my body. Even someone like me, someone who had built walls a mile thick around my heart, could most certainly feel this loss.

With Emma's death came the end of eight and a half years of chaotic, unconditional love.

A few months after Emma died, I quit my job as the marketing director for a bank holding company. I had worked there thirteen years, and the bank just didn't feel the same anymore after Emma's death. It hadn't felt the same for a long while, and I didn't realize until Emma was gone that *I* wasn't the same anymore, and I simply didn't belong there. I didn't want to deplete my energy there anymore.

"You've been running on empty for more than eight years keeping everything together for all of us," my husband said. "Now it's your turn to stop and breathe for a while." Although that sounded good in theory, I didn't know how to *actually stop and breathe* because my go-go-go, do-do-do self couldn't be still for long. I never learned how to *just be*. I wasn't comfortable with stillness, silence, or free time because that felt like wasted time. I experienced waves of guilt if I stopped to relax. I was accustomed to juggling many balls when Emma was with us, so that *quiet time* was uncomfortable.

At that time, I equated selfcare, rest, and relaxation to laziness, so I became very involved with several projects at Ian's school and in our community. Deadlines were my friend. Eventually, I found that I enjoyed being by myself while Corey was traveling during the week and Ian was at school. Perhaps always being surrounded by four siblings as a child and then having so many people in our home on a regular basis with Emma set me up for this new-found appreciation of solitude. It was a step in the right direction, but even so, in solitude, I was always busy and filled my alone time with do-do-doing endless tasks.

In time, I decided to throw myself into a big project that many of Emma's medical team had mentioned: an organization system to help families of chronically ill children keep track of *everything* (like the binder system we used in our home) so that multiple caregivers would have the information they needed at their fingertips. My brother Bradley helped me bring the EMMA System (Everyone's Medical Monitoring Assistant) to life. Unfortunately, the EMMA System launch happened simultaneously with new healthcare laws and looming insurance changes, so hospitals across the country had frozen their budgets.

When it became apparent that the EMMA System would not be distributed to families as I had hoped, I felt I had somehow failed Emma. It was hard enough losing her, but now I was missing her, *and* my vision for the EMMA System helping hundreds of chronically ill children and their families crumbled before my eyes.

Two things kept me moving into the future: I wanted happiness for my family and myself, and I believed it would be selfish of me to wish Emma back into her broken body. I knew without a doubt that she was free. Truly free. In my mind I could see her doing all the things she never got to do on earth—all those things in the dream my mom had a few days before she died. That dream had to be prophetic, a way for Emma to communicate with us that "everything would be okay." To genuinely believe in her freedom filled me with contentment and peace like nothing else ever had. My feelings of loss were fleeting, because I knew that Emma was happy and *complete* outside of her broken body.

My friend Sherri (who had the special Emma connection) continued to have unexpected moments with Emma even after she passed. She never truly understood what was happening, but she would contact me and let me know when something occurred. She said tears would always form in her eyes—not from sadness—but just out of the blue. She would see a hint of purplish-pink haze in her peripheral vision. Then she would have a very clear connection with Emma: a distinct thought, a clear message, a visual of some kind. She would call and share with me while everything was fresh in her mind. When Sherri had her own health scare and was hospitalized after a devastating car accident a few years after Emma's death, she was absolutely certain that Emma was with her in the car and in her hospital room on multiple occasions.

Over the years, there have been many Sherri-Emma connections, but one of the most incredible ones happened in December 2018 while Corey was recovering from hip replacement surgery. After Emma died, he usually slept with the oblong pillow that we used to prop up Emma's knees while *she* slept. In post-surgery loopiness, Corey would say, "Okay, now give me Emma," instead of "Emma's pillow." He made sure to have it right next to him in bed each night during his recovery.

Sherri sent me a text message the night of December 25, 2018, that said:

"Merry Christmas! This evening I have been blessed with Emma's presence. It's been a while and I've missed her. I've felt Emma with you, in particular over your left shoulder this evening. She loves you, Corey, and Ian. Hugs and kisses. She's enjoyed the pillow—not sure what that means or refers to, but some pillow with Corey or Ian and the dance with you in the hall/entry way."

While the other parts of her message also made sense, the pillow reference was clearly a gift. Every time Sherri tells me about an Emma connection, I soak it up and want to know all the details. They make me happy, but at the same time, I long for my own connections with Emma. Corey has had fairly regular experiences with her such as feeling Emma holding onto his feet or lying next to him. He says it is undeniably Emma. For me, I have only had limited encounters since Emma's death. When I have lain in bed at night, ready to drift off to sleep, I have felt Emma crawl into bed with me a handful of times. The first time it happened, I was a bit freaked out because this is something Emma could never have done while she was alive, but the physical sensation was something I had felt before when Ian had crawled into bed with me when he was a child.

That feeling of hand, knee, hand, knee lightly pressing into the mattress, moving from the bottom of the bed toward the pillows. It was real. Each time it happened, I would say, "Hey, Emma. Come on up here. I love you." There was nothing more to it. No visual, smell or temperature change. No tangible feeling on my skin. Just a nice, light feeling in my heart that she had come to see me in a way that I could physically sense. I knew that she was alive and well on the other side and she was playing and singing and dancing. I could see that in my mind. These unexpected moments were special and fleeting, like they were almost a tease. I wanted more than that. Sherri and Corey had more. I wondered why I couldn't have the same. I told some of my friends about these Emma connections, but only a couple of them embraced them at that time and many scoffed at the idea, so I became guarded about what I shared and with whom.

Corey and I discussed creating a butterfly garden in Emma's memory and did some research, hoping that something we could physically see and share with beautiful butterflies would keep us more connected with our missing butterfly. We couldn't seem to agree on a final plan, so we left it hanging on the to-do list for many years.

For a couple of years, a woman named Kim cleaned our house once a month. One day I came home from one of the Zumba classes I taught as she was cleaning the floor in the hall bathroom and, as I walked down the hallway, she yelled, "Oh! It's You!"

I had startled her, and I tilted my head and said, "Who did you think it would be?"

"Oh, well, um… nobody," she said a bit flustered, but not anxious.

At that moment, I could tell that she really did believe someone else was currently or had recently been in the house with her.

"Really, it's okay," I said, feeling cautiously optimistic that maybe, just maybe… "Who did you think it was? Was it Emma?"

Kim started telling me that this was not the first time she had felt someone in the house with her and that she was certain it was my daughter. (She shared that she had been "talking to dead people" since she was a little girl.) I asked what she saw or felt, and she said there was a light pinkish-purplish color in her visual field, and it was very strong today. Since she never knew Emma, she asked if it was close to a significant day, and I told her it was almost Emma's birthday. She confirmed that a birthday could be the reason her presence was so strong, but there was also another feeling that was clearly coming through, and she could tell that Emma was very concerned about her dad and that he needed to take care of himself. She asked if that made any sense at all, and I said that it did.

What Kim didn't know was that Corey had been working as a consultant on an out-of-state project for a few years, and for the last six months, he had been working ten to twelve hours a day, seven days a week without a break. The stress and exhaustion were taking a major toll on his health, and I was concerned that he would end up hospitalized – or worse. Kim's message from Emma helped to shine a light on the severity of the situation and helped Corey understand that he would need to address it with his employer. Soon after Kim's revelation, Corey found himself recovering from medical complications directly stemming from high stress, resulting in a change not only in Corey's mindset about his job but also with his employer and setting more realistic expectations. Emma had his back the whole way, yet I was left wishing that she would connect with me directly because I longed for that clear, close, physical evidence of her "beingness" with me.

Not long after Kim shared Emma's message for her dad, she and her family moved out of the area, and then a year later, she called unexpectedly and asked if she could come to the house to see me. When she arrived, she said that Emma had clearly "asked her to get some things for me" and she couldn't ignore Emma's request: a pair of earrings in a store where she was shopping and a small butterfly bush. She had no idea why, but she had to get these things to me right away.

Corey and I had just been discussing removing a half wall

in front of our house and possibly, *finally*, putting in Emma's Butterfly Garden. We hadn't made any definite plans yet, but when Kim handed me the butterfly bush, I knew it was time. Emma basically told us to stop stalling. We walked outside to the front of the house, and I showed Kim where we were considering removing the wall and putting in the garden, and I told her about our procrastination with the butterfly garden plans. She breathed in a slow, deep breath.

"Yes, this is it," she said nodding. "Emma actually gave me the plan if you'd like me to draw it out for you."

I laughed and said, "Sure!"

Just then, a butterfly flew in front of us, and we knew it was right.

In 2017, I saw a holistic therapist in St. Louis for knee and shoulder pain from overusing my body without proper sleep for repair and regeneration (yes, I still had sleep problems). Malina was a friend who was known for her special healing gifts. She had extensive training in multiple modalities, including similar energy techniques as those of my friend Sherri's.

While on Malina's table, I was mesmerized by her ability to feel energy flows and to pinpoint areas in my body that were constricted, in pain or inflamed even without directly touching those areas. We talked extensively about these natural talents, which she considered gifts from God. Our conversation then turned to the energy of our loved ones, past and present, and how she could feel that energy, too. She mentioned her deceased loved one visiting her through electricity with flickering lights in her home and radios playing very specific songs when she turned to a station. I felt confident sharing information about my sporadic (and too few) nighttime "visits" from Emma and admitted that I wished to have a better connection with my daughter. She asked if

I had ever read Anita Moorjani's book *Dying to Be Me,* or if I had seen her TED Talk. I wasn't familiar with either but was drawn in when I learned more about Anita's story.

Anita Moorjani suffered from cancer for years. In her last moments of life, with lemon-size tumors throughout her body, she was in a coma and her organs were shutting down. She went to the "other side" and met with her father's essence (his soul), a man with whom she had a contentious relationship while he was living. She was also enveloped by her best friend's essence. Her best friend had died of cancer and that illness had significantly increased Anita's fear of the disease, which is what she was dying of at that moment. Each being with whom she connected was an extension of pure, unconditional love, and she knew they were infinite. She was given the option of returning to her body, knowing she would be healed, or crossing over permanently. She returned to her physical body and fully recovered within a couple of months and is healthy and thriving today, sharing her story and inspiring people to live and love fully and fearlessly, shining their own lights into the world because love (which includes all our loved ones, everyONE and everyTHING) is unconditional on the other side, but also right here with us if we are willing to accept it.

As Moorjani says in *Dying to Be Me,* Chapter 7: "I had unlimited perception...365-degree peripheral vision with total awareness of my surroundings...my heightened awareness in that expanded realm was indescribable...the clarity was amazing... I saw my life intricately woven into everything I'd known so far. My experience was like a single thread woven through the huge and complexly colorful images of an infinite tapestry. All the other threads and colors represented my relationships including every life I'd touched...to create the fabric that was the sum of my life up to this point...I became aware that we're all connected... everything in the universe...everything belongs to an infinite whole...we are all one."

Moorjani continues in Chapter 8: "Imagine if you will a huge, dark warehouse. You live there with only one flashlight to see by. Everything you know...is what you've seen by the beam of one small flashlight. Whenever you want to look for something, you may or may not find it, but that doesn't mean the thing doesn't exist. It's there, but you just haven't shone your light on it...you can only see what your light is focused on and only identify that which you already know...that is what physical life is like...Next, imagine that one day someone flicks on a switch. There for the first time in a sudden burst of brilliance in sound and color, you can see the entire warehouse and it's nothing like anything you've ever imagined...the vastness, complexity, depth and breadth of everything going on around you is almost overwhelming. You can't see all the way to the end of the space and you know there's more to it than what you can take in...You understand that what you used to think was your reality was in fact hardly a speck within the vast wonder that surrounds you...so even when the switch goes back off, nothing can take away your understanding and clarity and the wonder and beauty...Nothing can ever cancel your knowledge of all that exists in the warehouse...You're left with a sense of awe."

This understanding that even when we can't see, hear, feel, smell or taste something, it still exists, even our loved ones like my Emma - boom. I thought that was true. I wanted that to be true. I had hoped it was true. Now it was making more sense and really connected me to Emma knowing that she was literally right here, right there, everywhere, in a state of wonder and awe. Call it Heaven. Call it the other side. Call it whatever resonates with you, but for me, Heaven became so much more real and present. Not something that was waiting for me when I died, but seriously existing in the now and forever, surrounded by all of God's love, yet being part of God at the same time. Emma was and is there and experiencing everything in the most amazing way, surrounded by all-encompassing, unconditional love that doesn't look back and is nothing like we can even imagine. That is what made so much sense to me. No judgment, just love.

Reading about Moorjani's near-death experience (NDE) helped me to sort out feelings I had been having and limitations I had put on God. It felt so wrong for me to keep God – and Jesus - in a box with all kinds of rules and man-made, fear-based constraints, being judged and judging others for the level of adherence to the "rules." My God was so much bigger than that, so much more loving and so full of grace. Knowing. Really *knowing* that Emma was part of the everlasting everything right now (and I didn't have to wait until my body gave out to have that connection with her again) made so much more sense to me than anything ever had. I knew about people who had NDEs, and I had heard many stories about people having "visits" of some kind from their loved ones after death, but because I had been taught that these things couldn't possibly be true or they were wrong somehow, I had been fighting an internal battle with these beliefs.

My eyes and heart were opening to a much broader understanding of what truly made sense as *my* truth. Things I had been struggling with for years started making more sense. Here on earth, we put an awful lot of pressure on each other to live how we decide they should live, and not at all based on the acceptance and love that God has for all of us as part of the Creator. Opening my mind and heart made it so much clearer that Emma was whole and happy and that because the separation between me and her was more of a restriction I had created, I wanted to understand how to have a stronger connection with her. I wanted her to "visit" me in more tangible ways. There would be a difference between believing and having a physical knowing.

I started noticing more how the energy around other people affected me, and I gave myself permission to remove myself from situations that felt like energy vampires sucking the life out of me. I became acutely aware of the drama that can easily overtake people's lives, and how so much of that drama is self-created and then shared with others to infect and spread. I began blocking a lot of drama from myself by changing the subject or by simply asking someone who starts sharing the latest gossip with me if it is their story to share. If it's not, then I just tell that person that I don't want to hear it. It became apparent to me that when I focused on happiness and joy and made a conscious decision to invite those positive aspects into my life, I had a much greater chance of experiencing that during the day.

Life was continuing to get calmer, happier, richer, but I still had some concerns tugging at me. Even with all the years that had passed since Emma's death, my sleep was still very light and extremely interrupted. Trying all the "sleep aid" tricks and tips didn't change it. I am still working on this today. I still wake up multiple times at night and just stare into space while lying still or trying to talk myself into sleep with my eyes closed. I can't remember the last time I slept through the night. I had made many improvements in my personal care and was doing a lot of things "right" for myself: nutrition, exercise, selfcare and personal growth, but I could not get the sleep part of the equation figured out. It was taking a toll on me because my body simply cannot repair properly without good sleep. As healthy as I was, I was becoming exhausted and felt like my body was giving out. Trying to unlock the mystery to my sleep disorder is an ongoing project, but I also had another issue that was unresolved. I knew in my heart that Emma was happy I was finding balance in my life, but I still wanted that physical connection. Something "real" and earthly that I could see or feel or smell or taste that would be without a doubt *her*.

I was on a dual quest for sleep and connection, and the most fascinating things occurred in the span of about six months.

When I heard that a chiropractor in town was trained in acupuncture, I made an appointment hoping it could help me sleep better. During my appointment, she shared a lot of information about acupuncture points and energy pathways in the body and

I got this *feeling* about her. I couldn't really explain it, but I said, "Doc, do you see colors?" She got a funny look on her face and said, "Why do you ask that?" I told her I just had this feeling that she could see colors, auras (the energy field surrounding each of us that expands outward a few feet from our bodies). She replied, "I don't tell people that, but yes." Ohhhhhh, I was so excited! I told her I had been wondering what color my aura was - I specifically wanted to know what my energy field looked like. She chuckled and said, "It's bright red. Fiery red." I said, "And that's a good thing, right?" Again, she kind of chuckled and said that because she knew me and my personality, it just made sense, but that for someone who doesn't sleep, I may want to consider adding more of the color *blue* to my life to calm down some of that red. She asked me what color the rooms are in my home. I told her that I have a big red wall in my bedroom. She laughed again and said, "When you remodel, you may want to consider painting your room a nice, calm color like blue." We also talked about red being my favorite color throughout my life. Seeing auras and talking about them is not part of her medical practice, but since I asked, she answered. She said she had been able to see colors around people her whole life. When she was a little girl, she asked her mom why different people had different colors around them, and her mom had no idea what she was talking about. She also said that it can be quite draining to be in public places because she can see everyone's auras - including those that are very sick. I was fascinated, and every time I see her, I ask her what color I am that day. I'm always particularly pleased when I am a rose pink or muted red.

These encounters with my chiropractor helped me learn more about the energy pulsing through my body and how it affects how I feel and how I manage life in general, but it also opened more opportunity for me to understand energy around me. Knowing that Emma's energy was literally around me, too, this motivated me to be as open as possible to any connection that could happen.

Lying still and focusing on my breath while the acupuncture needles do their thing allows me more time to just "be" so that my heart can be more receptive.

A couple of weeks after one of my acupuncture appointments, my friend Sherri stopped by my house while another mutual friend was there. Our mutual friend asked Sherri about scheduling time with her for lymphatic drainage, and Sherri immediately laid her hands on our friend and said, "Yes, I see that you need it." Within just a few short moments, there was a noticeable improvement in the swollen area. They chatted briefly and then I said to Sherri, "Okay, now me!" She kind of chuckle-sighed and said, "Okay. I'll try."

Sherri walked over to me and put her hands on me, but then she stepped back and said, "I can't do it. Emma is right here." She pointed to my chest. Since I was wearing a necklace with a picture of Emma in the pendant, I said, "Oh, I can take off the Emma necklace." She laughed and said, "No, it's not the necklace. It's Emma. Can you not *feel* that? Can you not *feel* her? She is right *here*." She touched my chest and then waved her hand in the space right in front of me.

I said, "No. I can't feel it. I can't feel her. I don't understand why not." I was deflated and confused.

We scheduled a time for Sherri to come to the house a few days later to work on Corey and on me for...whatever might happen. She never touched Corey's skin, but she used her hands to move energy in Corey's body, and it helped him immensely. He could feel all of it. I just watched and was amazed that Corey was always so in tune with this process. It was second nature for him to feel it. Then it was my turn. Sherri came to my side and tried, but again, she said she couldn't because Emma was "right here." She waved her arms in front of me as I was lying still. I was frustrated and discouraged that I couldn't feel her. Sherri asked me to lie still with my eyes closed. My arms were to my sides. She asked me to just lie still without trying to "do" anything and to tell her if I felt anything. After a few minutes, I told her I felt like the hair on my left forearm and wrist was standing up and that part of my arm was quite cold and tingling.

"That's Emma!" she said. "Her hand is literally touching you there!"

I opened my eyes and saw that Sherri's hand was hovering about three inches above my arm and wrist, but she was *not* touching me. Finally, I could feel that physical connection. I was peaceful. It didn't necessarily feel like *Emma*, but it was something real. Sherri reminded me that Emma is always with me and that I just need to "let go" to let her in.

A couple of weeks later, I found out there was an online course that Anita Moorjani was teaching, so I joined about six hundred people from around the world to listen with an open mind and heart. At the end of one of the live Zoom lessons, we had the option to stay on for a smaller group activity. When I opted to stay, I was moved into a group of five women from all over the world. Our assignment was to take turns giving and receiving energy. In the back of my mind, I was thinking, "Oh, great. This should be interesting." I already knew I could *give*, but I had a problem *receiving*. In addition, while I knew that everything was energy, I was having a lot of difficulty visualizing anything that wasn't physically manifested in a five-senses type scenario. I was going to give it my best try, though.

We took turns saying what we wanted energy for. I asked for energy to sleep through the night. The other women shared their wishes. After we all had our receiving sessions, we each shared our experience from the receiving end and then the others shared their experience on the giving end for us. When it was my turn, I told the group that I didn't think I did it right because I didn't feel anything when I was in the receiving mode, and I tried really hard to send energy to each woman, but I couldn't necessarily see or feel anything. The other women shared their experiences of sending/giving to me. The first woman who was from an eastern European country said that when she started sending energy to me, she felt like she should send me a rainbow of colors and light, but that she immediately hit a wall and had to "bore through it with a bright blue light." I thought of my chiropractor's recommendation to get more "blue" into my life, and I chuckled and said, "Well, that makes sense." Then another woman from a European country said, "Julie, when I sent you energy, all I could see was red fire and volcanoes." I laughed out loud when I heard that and said, "Yep, that makes sense, too." Then I told the group about my fiery red aura and my need for more blue in my life.

I was rather amazed by this experience, but then during the last live class, I was in for a treat. I was one of the people who got to speak with Anita directly on the webinar, live in front of more than six hundred global participants. I told her about my difficulty in visualizing things and that I was trying to learn how to connect with my daughter. Anita said, "Your daughter has passed to the other side, hasn't she?" When I told her yes, she asked me to give her the background information. She said, "She is right there with you, you just need to quit trying so hard and let go so that she can get in." It was the same message I was hearing from numerous sources, most recently from my friend Sherri. It was my ingrained behavior of do-do-doing getting in the way of be-be-being in connection with Emma.

The following week, as I was waiting in my driveway for my garage door to open, I looked to my left at Emma's Butterfly Garden. It was a bright, cheerful, summer morning and the flowers were blooming.

"Okay, Emma," I said out loud. "Send me a butterfly or something, *please*. Something I can see. Okay?"

The garage door opened, I parked the car, and went into the house for a few minutes to get something before heading out to another appointment. An hour later I was in the driveway again waiting for the garage door to open, and again I looked to my left toward the garden. I saw a white butterfly flying around the blooms. At first, I didn't think much about it, because there were often white butterflies in the garden. Then it dawned on me that the white butterflies are usually there in the afternoon, not in the morning. At that moment, that single white butterfly flew straight at me, stopped about six inches from the side car window—right in front of my face—for a few seconds, and then flew away. "Well, okay then, Emma!" I said, laughing. "I saw you! Now do it again." I went inside the house, feeling light and happy, and oh-so-connected, but I didn't see another butterfly-specific message from Emma.

A few weeks later, I saw a friend's post on Facebook that elicited an immediate physical response. Lisa was a high school acquaintance, and she had posted a picture of her daughter, Mallory, in a wheelchair and all bundled up at the Cleveland Clinic. They were leaving after a fact-finding mission to try to pinpoint Mallory's medical problems and how to fix them. I didn't really know Lisa, as she was a few years ahead of me in school, and we hadn't really spoken or seen each other since high school, but we had that Facebook connection. I had seen many parents post pictures of their sick children over the years, but for some reason I was really drawn to Mallory. She looked like she was in her twenties, but it was hard to tell since she was so bundled up in the middle of summer. My heart usually connected with pictures or stories of younger kids who were sick or undergoing treatments of some kind, but Mallory's story stuck.

I connected with Lisa and learned about Mallory's medical history and the continued mystery surrounding her situation, and I offered what little help I could. Then Lisa mentioned Mallory's "psychic abilities" and I felt a bolt of excitement rush through my body. It felt like Mallory could be a connecting point for Emma. Lisa suggested that Corey and I meet Mallory in person the next time we were in their area (about three hours away) if she was feeling up to it.

Within a few minutes after disconnecting with Lisa, Corey called from Kansas City. He had just reconnected with a friend he hadn't seen in years, and his eagerness to share his story was just as palpable as mine. His friend's thirty-year-old son had died six years before, and she and her daughter had struggled a lot after his death until they connected with a psychic who was able to send messages from him. It was an entirely overwhelming experience because there was no possible way for the psychic to have known what he shared with them. It was very personal, private information that came through—so that both the mom and sister would know, without a doubt, that it was a real connection, resulting in peace.

Corey's friend had suggested that I find someone to help Emma connect with us and we should trust that the universe (AKA God) will provide the right person. I then gave Corey a quick recap of my conversation with Lisa and Corey said, "If that isn't God telling you Mallory might be that person, I don't know how much clearer it could be."

Within a couple of months, we were in Mallory's area and meeting with this beautiful young woman who was propped up on pillows in her bed. The three of us talked for a little while and then she insisted on doing a reading for us. Mallory requested ice packs from her mom, as her body had started to heat up significantly. She pulled out a deck of angel cards and began to shuffle, and Corey commented that he was so intrigued by my openness since I had been so "black and white" all my life. He told her he hoped I could recognize how many grey areas there were in life.

Mallory pulled the first angel card, and it featured a picture of a zebra with the words: *Not everything is black and white.* That made all of us laugh, of course. The next few cards were similarly powerful and had very personal messages for me that Mallory couldn't have known about. I was in awe of the whole experience, and I felt so much love from Mallory. There was nothing scary or strange about the meeting because all we could feel from her was pure love from an open heart, like God was giving us information *through her* that we needed.

About a week later, Mallory and I met on a Zoom call so that she could share what she experienced during a concentrated meditation on my behalf. At that point, the only information that Mallory had about Emma was that she had died.

What she shared with me was nothing short of amazing. Mallory said Emma was very young when she died (she was eight). When Mallory asked Emma through the meditation to confirm how she passed, Mallory started coughing as if she were choking and then she touched her throat. She was having trouble breathing and talking, but Mallory said that it felt like there was something in her throat. It was a strong sensation in her throat, like she needed to cough and wanted to take a deep breath. For some reason, it didn't feel like she had a problem with her lungs, though. It felt like there was something rigid in her throat, like a tube.

My eyes were wide, and I had goosebumps. When Mallory asked if this made any sense to me, and I told her it made perfect sense, and I described Emma's last day on earth.

Mallory continued to share: Emma was a little girl, and she was sitting in a wheelchair. She saw a lot of pink, and that Emma wore pink and purple clothes... but there was one thing that Mallory shared about her meditation that didn't make sense to me. She kept getting the number three from Emma. She asked if it could be in reference to the number of family members, number of kids—or something like that?

"Maybe it was that there were three of us left: me, Corey, Ian," I said, not quite certain. She said, "Whatever "three" is, it's very strong. It must mean something."

Later that evening, when I told Corey about our call and all the things Mallory shared, including my confusion about the number three, he immediately reacted and said, "Julie, of course!

Three! I. LOVE. YOU. It's how Emma and I told each other I LOVE YOU. Blink. Blink. Blink. One. Two. Three."

At this point, many of my friends and acquaintances might believe I've "gone off the rails" and have been possessed or something. They might even think I have crossed over to the "dark side," but I can say with absolute certainty that this is not the case. Every interaction I have had with people who have extraordinary gifts are the kindest, most loving people I've met, and they definitely have a direct connection with God. I believe with my whole heart that they are people I was supposed to meet and were placed in my path to help me understand that life doesn't get colored within the lines. I needed to really learn through experience that there is always more than what is right before us, and that God is so much more amazing in all ways and always. I had to be open to the colors around the edges and I had to be willing to stop and just *be* for Emma to *be with me* again. Everything has been surrounded by pure love, and that's what God is to me. God is love.

The world came to a screeching halt in March 2020 due to the Covid pandemic. Almost immediately I found myself with a lot of extra time for *nothing*. My very busy schedule packed with business, family and social events turned into blank calendar squares. There was a lot less time to focus on the do-do-doing of life and I now had more opportunities than ever to just *be*, whether I liked it or not. Those two years of life-as-we-never-knew-it made me reflect on my priorities and how much I crammed into each day. I learned that I really needed to be around people and share that social energy with others, but that I didn't need to be "busy" all the time and truly enjoyed the quiet times at home more than I thought I ever could. I started focusing more on expanding my human BEING-ness instead of my human DOING-ness in hopes of another connection with Emma.

The day before Thanksgiving 2021 I was in the kitchen all day preparing food. I was really missing Emma, so I just said out loud, "Okay, Emma, are you here? Are you with me? If you are, let me know. Give me a sign." It was way too cold to see a butterfly, so I wasn't sure what she would or could do.

I wanted some background noise while cooking, so I chose a random movie titled HERE TODAY with Billy Crystal. His character suffers from dementia, and he meets a woman named Emma who becomes his caregiver. I thought to myself, "Okay, Emma, that was pretty good." The next random movie was FINDING YOU. The main character goes to Ireland for a semester abroad and her host family meets her at the Dublin airport. The teenage girl of the family runs up to her and gives her a big hug, saying, "I'm your new sister Emma!" I chuckled and said, "Okay, Emma, you did it again."

Then we had family here for Thanksgiving and after everyone left, Corey and I started decorating for Christmas. I chose a random Christmas themed movie from the "new" category and in the first thirty seconds of the movie, the main character is doing a voice-over as an author talking about her best-selling books. She says, "...those were the words that started the whole Emma Gale success story" talking about her famous character Emma who spanned all her books. I laughed out loud and went to get Corey and made him listen to the introduction because I had told him about the other two "Emma things."

Within the next two weeks I met a young mother who had her son with her and a baby girl in a car seat carrier. I asked the boy what his baby sister's name was, and he said, "Socks!" The mom said, "He always calls her "Socks" for some reason, but her name is Emma." I told her my baby girl's name is Emma and then later that night I heard the movie THE MAP OF TINY PERFECT THINGS playing in the other room. The main character's sister's name in that movie is, of course, *Emma*. I was getting her message. She was there with me for sure.

When a child dies before the parents, the natural timeline is broken. I remember meeting my father-in-law's mother for the first time. I was pregnant with Emma. Grandma Powers was in her early eighties at the time and had lost her son, (Corey's father), three years before. When Corey talked about his father with Grandma Powers, I remember her saying something that day that stuck with me: "It doesn't matter how old you are and how old your child is, if your child dies before you do, it's just not natural and it's too hard to accept." It was eye opening to realize that my father-in-law was her child, her baby, even if he had been in his sixties. He had died before his mom, and I remember feeling that the loss of a child would be dreadful, whether that child is a baby, child, teen, adult, or senior citizen. I had no idea what was waiting for me in my future.

Yet here I am, the mother of a dead daughter. The good news is that I know two things about Emma: (1) She came to earth for a purpose (which she completed, and I played a prominent role), and (2) she isn't *actually dead*. She's alive and well and living within the best of everything, and one day I will experience all that she is with her, alongside her. I can talk to her, and occasionally she sends messages back that I can understand. I'm getting better at *letting go* so that I can *allow in* and experience these messages. If that seems difficult to wrap your head around, I get it. Sometimes things don't make sense until we have a personal experience because fear and heartbreak keep us from being open to possibilities.

When I meet new people and I'm asked about my family and how many kids I have, I say that I have two kids. I say that my son is all grown up and living a life of adventure in Colorado, and my daughter is forever eight years old and living an existence beyond imagination in the ever-after of Heaven. Usually, I get a confused look quickly followed by a sad look and then a stammering apology for saying anything. I tell them it's okay because I know Emma is right here with me. Her energy continues.

Everything is energy and energy cannot be destroyed. It simply changes form. Emma has changed form, and her energy is in a new "space." I miss having her where I can see her and touch her and smell her, but knowing she was here *and she mattered* is important, and I like to talk about her. I like for people to remember her.

A resource I discovered during the Covid pandemic lockdown helped put this whole view into even clearer perspective. Suzanne Giesemann is a retired U.S. Navy Commander, author, speaker, teacher, evidential medium and major supporter of the organization Helping Parents Heal. Her personal story is unexpected but powerful. She experienced extreme loss on 9/11 while serving as the aide to the Chairman of the Joint Chiefs of Staff and was in the last plane to fly over the Twin Towers in New York before returning to the Pentagon where death and destruction awaited her. Then she lost her stepdaughter (who was pregnant with her first baby) to a lightning strike on her marine base. After these events, Suzanne started searching outside her left-brain logical self for answers to questions like, "Is this really all there is?" and "What happens after we die?" Her experiences after asking these questions took a surprising turn when she developed her mediumship. Her books, videos, podcasts, and daily inspirational messages bring many fuzzy things into clarity, especially those that feature parents who have lost children from all causes and at all ages. Every message she shares is filled with love: radiant love and reminders that we are all here to allow the light of our souls to shine.

While those in the scientific fields agree that energy cannot be created or destroyed and that it can only be changed from one form to another, "science" has yet to explain how the energy of a soul, the spark of life that makes someone into a specific human, moves out of the body at "death" and what type of energy remains or *how* it is transformed. And then there's Quantum Entanglement, or what Albert Einstein referred to as "spooky action at a distance." It's a phenomenon by which one particle can basically "know" something about another particle instantaneously and even *change the properties* of another object (even at great distances apart). Two particles, separated by light years, can be connected by a mysterious communication channel. I'm pretty sure that Emma and I are entangled at the quantum level. At the soul level.

In the last decade, scientific measurements have become more sensitive to measuring the energy within and surrounding life forms. There are even machines that can basically measure someone's "aura" now as well as how emotional stimuli impact the body's energy flow and resulting wellness or disease. Scientifically measured. Not "woo woo-lly" felt. I'm amazed and intrigued by these things, and I believe that what scientists are "discovering" now are things that have been known for literally thousands of years in ancient cultures.

In my years on the planet, I've been honored to meet many people with highly developed natural gifts who understand these things that "science" will one day recognize. These amazing people have been instrumental in my understanding of connecting with Emma as well as the body's energy centers and how they get out of alignment, how my energy flows *within* my body, how it radiates outward from my body, and how my emotions affect the energy flow and vice versa. I've also learned a lot about how others' energy affects mine in ways I never realized. These energy healers have helped me pinpoint areas of concern and paths to healing. Every single one of these people is filled with love and humble appreciation for their connections with God and the guidance of the Creator of all energy, and I have so much gratitude for their helping hearts.

I don't want to give anyone the false assumption that I've figured it all out and that I live in a land of high energy rainbows and joyful sunshine, good times, music, laughter and dance every single day. Things get hard sometimes. I get overwhelmed, and now that I'm allowing myself to *truly feel* more often, those feelings really do wash over me and can knock me off my feet.

When things around me seem to be falling apart, and when my own body seems to betray me, I just want to curl up and hide or run away somewhere "safe." Dancing has moments of missteps before the rhythm falls into sync again.

Some days are harder than others because this lifelong sleep issue has meant that my body has never really had a chance to repair and regenerate each night like it's supposed to, so my body has suffered from some funky and "not yet diagnosed" problem areas that I just "deal with." For all the bizarre things that make medical professionals go "Hmmm…" I simply throw them into the "Weirdness of Julie (WOJ)" category and go on with life as best I can by controlling what I can, like what's on the end of my fork and the people with whom I surround myself. I know that all things aren't black and white, so those grey areas will just be grey until there are answers.

The best ways I can think to honor Emma are to create my best life possible and bring as much light and love into the world that I can. I feel in my heart, my bones, and my soul that Emma wants to see me, her family and everyone happy and whole and; it feels to me, that life on the *other side* is even better when more light from this side shines over there. Being my truest self and not someone other people have constructed is the most authentic way to shine. I am on a path to discover my authentic self and my true purpose in the world. One way I do this is through quieting my mind in the morning and asking God, "What do I need to know today?" and "How can I be of service today?" I ask how I can impact the world in the best way possible and who needs what I have to offer.

There are parents (as well as others) who are suffering with grief, and the loss is new or decades long. It doesn't matter because grieving has no timeline. My prayer is that each person will find a way to continue taking steps into the future and toward the true light of our Creator with memories of loved ones warming the heart. When we ask ourselves what brings us joy and carve out time to experience that joy, it makes a difference. I've learned how important it is that the joy, happiness, contentment, and peace I feel is truly within so that it can radiate from the inside out versus searching for these things outside of myself. Specific achievements, vacations, possessions won't bring any true and lasting joy. It's what we do to spread love and light in the world that matters. Our Creator filled our souls with love. It's our job to spread it around and make this earthly experience the best it can possibly be for everyone.

My prayer is that I can continue to live my best life so that I can help people live their best lives through my fitness classes (Zumba), my functional food nutritional support (Juice Plus+), the vertical growing system allowing people to grow their own fresh food year-round (Tower Garden by Juice Plus+), and recorded conversations I capture for my Happy Cells and Souls program (Facebook and YouTube). My mission is to create better health at the CELLular level and more joy at the SOULular level.

My daily goals include:

Take long, slow, deep breaths.
Feel the feelings, acknowledge them.
Shine brightly enough to ignite others.
Love fully.
Make choices based on love, not fear.
Listen more, talk less.
Collect friends who I value and who value me for *me*.
Judge people less, accept differences more.
See things from multiple perspectives.
Grant grace, remembering that people are doing the best they can.
Refrain from assumptions and writing other people's stories.
Understand what resonates with my inner being.
Learn as much as possible from all kinds of people.
Encourage and inspire.

Emma taught me a lot while she was here with me in physical form, but she has taught me so much more since she left her body behind. I must be open to the lessons. I'm certain she fulfilled her personal mission while she was having her physical experience and continues from the realm of Heaven. (I was recently told that she is serving as Director of my "creative team," which makes me smile.)

While Emma's story here on earth had a physical beginning and end, you and I are still here to continue our stories. Let's make them count.

HELPFUL RESOURCES:

www.anitamoorjani.com
   Book: Dying to Be Me

www.helpingparentsheal.org
   Documentary: Life to Afterlife: Mom Can You Hear Me

www.suzannegiesemann.com
   Books: Messages of Hope, the Priest and the Medium, Wolf's Message and Droplets of God

ABOUT THE AUTHOR: JULIE POWERS

 Julie Powers is a functional food and aeroponic gardening educator, an affiliate with the Juice Plus+ Company since 2013, a licensed Zumba instructor since 2011 and the creator of Happy Cells and Souls (a video channel on Facebook and YouTube). Julie's mission is to create better health at the CELLular level and more joy at the SOULular level while being a friend collector and connector. Helping other parents who have outlived their children find light through their darkness is a particular focus for her.

Website: happycellsandsouls.com
Facebook: Julie Ross Powers / Julie Powers – Happy Cells and Souls
Instagram: Julie Ross Powers
Email: jpowers.happycellsandsouls@gmail.com
Juice Plus+ Whole Food Nutrition: jpowers.juiceplus.com
Tower Garden by Juice Plus+: jpowers.towergarden.com
Zumba: https://www.zumba.com/en-US/p/julie-powers/142712